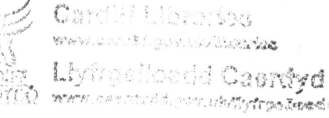

Promoting Children's Rights in Social Work and Social Care

A Guide to Participatory Practice

D1556298

Margaret Bell

Foreword by Mary John

Jessica Kingsley *Publishers*
London and Philadelphia

First published in 2011
by Jessica Kingsley Publishers
116 Pentonville Road
London N1 9JB, UK
and
400 Market Street, Suite 400
Philadelphia, PA 19106, USA

www.jkp.com

Library of Congress Cataloging in Publication Data
Bell, Margaret, 1945-
  Promoting children's rights in social work and social care : a guide to
participatory practice / Margaret Bell ; foreword by Mary John.
       p. cm.
  Includes bibliographical references and index.
  ISBN 978-1-84310-607-4 (alk. paper)
  1. Children's rights--Great Britain. 2. Social work with children--Great
Britain. 3. Child welfare--Government policy--Great Britain. I. Title.
  HQ789.B45 2011
  362.7--dc22
                                    2011004523

British Library Cataloguing in Publication Data
A CIP catalogue record for this book is available from the British Library

ISBN 978 1 84310 607 4

Printed and bound in Great Britain

Contents

Series Editor's Foreword

As someone who has been involved in advocating children's rights for many years now, I am conscious of the long hard journey that it has been for children and those supporting them since I and fellow advocates all gathered together at the World Conference on Research and Practice in Children's Rights held at the University of Exeter from 8–11 September, 1992.

At that event, we started to take stock of the responses there had been to the UN Convention on the Rights of the Child and whether the activities that had followed had facilitated the involvement of children, and, if so, the ways in which they had been empowering. At that point in time, we realised that we had a long way to go.

The 'Children in Charge' book series was originally conceived to help promote research, good policy and best practice in promoting children's rights as outlined in the UN Convention, and its titles have reflected a shift over time – starting optimistically with *Children in Charge: The Child's Right to a Fair Hearing* (John 1996a) and *Children in Our Charge: The Child's Right to Resources* (John 1996b), then the combatively titled *A Charge Against Society: Children's Right to Protection* (John 1997).

We have subsequently featured books dedicated to exploring the implications of the UN Convention for different areas of practice – working with traveller children (Kiddle 1999), children's rights in education (Hart *et al.* 2001), and children's rights in early years (Alderson 2008). It has been heartening to see many of the ideas which originated within the movement being integrated within society – within politics, our shared communal values and professional practice.

Commonly expressed concerns about importance of wellbeing and happiness among children and the population at large also echo concerns that have been raised by the children's rights movement for many years.

I'm very pleased that the important subject of children's rights in social work and social care is now being addressed by the series in this new book by Margaret Bell.

It comes at a timely moment, as children's voices have been heard in street demonstrations making clear their views and their right to resources, and indeed in a special session in the House of Commons (House of Commons 2010). At the same time, social workers are required to recognise the rights of children but also face challenges in their own work and resources.

What Margaret Bell describes here is the theory and practice of truly vanguard work on how to keep children informed and important in matters which concern them and ultimately our whole society.

Mary John
Professor Emeritus, Exeter University

Acknowledgements

My desire to write a book about children's participation in social work is rooted in my own practice and teaching on social work with children and families, and the research I have done with children and families on their experiences of involvement in their social work.

I am indebted to my colleagues at the University of York for the work we have done together over the last decade on the research studies presented in Part II of this book: Jon Somerton on child protection investigations, Terry Fisher on parenting programmes, Kate Wilson on family group conferences and the R U Being Heard project, and finally Ian Shaw, Ian Sinclair, Paul Dyson, Tricia Sloper and Wendy Mitchell on the Integrated Children's System. Without funding none of these studies would have been possible, for which thanks to the Joseph Rowntree Foundation, the Department of Health and Department for Children, Schools and Families and the Cities of York and Kingston upon Hull.

Stephen Jones at Jessica Kingsley deserves thanks for his patience and helpful suggestions on the writing of the book. And thanks, also, to my family and friends for their love, support and encouragement.

Lastly, thanks go to all the children and young people who have given of themselves and their time to talk about experiences which have often been sad and difficult, but whose words and thoughts tell us what social workers can do to help them to exert their right to be involved in decisions about their lives.

Introduction

This book attempts to do three things: to explain and explore the foundations of children's participation in decisions that affect them, to describe some children's experiences of involvement in individual and organisational arenas, and to identify the values, skills and knowledge which practitioners and their employers need to effect empowering practice.

Children's rights to participate in the decision-making process are enshrined in Article 12 of the United Nations Convention on the Rights of the Child (UNCRC) (United Nations 1989). Article 12 grants a child who is capable of forming a view the right to express that view freely in all matters affecting him, and these views should be given due weight in accordance with the age and maturity of the child.

So, for most practitioners and their agencies and the organisations involved the question now is not what to do or whether to do it, but how. This book, and the research studies presented, illustrate what works and what gets in the way. It should therefore be of use to practitioners working with children, their managers who set up the structures to enable children's participation to happen and to students and academics who are interested in the policy and theories underpinning the thinking and recent developments in participatory practice.

In the UK, the Children Act (1989) was the main driver in requiring the involvement of children and young people in a range of decision-making arenas, the focus at that time being on their involvement in individual social work decision-making arenas. Subsequent legislation and guidance continues to encourage the rights of children to participate, the focus now being more on enabling their involvement in organisational policy and change. *Every Child Matters* (Department for Education and Skills (DfES) 2004a, 2004b) based its overall goals for achievement on the five outcomes on consultations with children, and the Children Act (2004), contained legislation to further children's participation in advising on new local authority structures, such as Children's Trusts. A Children's Commissioner for England was created with the intention of ensuring children's rights are upheld and their voices heard in a range of arenas. Further opportunities for participation, especially in schools, were named in the 2007 Children's Plan, *Building Brighter Futures* (Department for Children, Schools and Families (DCSF) 2007b), which set out strategic objectives for the next ten years.

While the structures for enabling children to participate in organisations, in particular schools and youth forums, are improving there is less evidence that children are routinely involved in decision making at an individual level in social work, such as in assessments, in writing their records or in meetings. And there continues to be debate about how children's rights should be exercised both by children in groups, and by children as individuals. While there is generally agreement that the nature and degree of children's participation, both in policy and in the process of practice in the UK, will vary depending on the child's interest, capacity and the decisions to be made, there are continuing concerns not just about the difficulties in process but also about definitions and, indeed, about the generality of the principle itself. On the one hand, there is a move to see children as individuals and social actors with capacity for self realisation; on the other, there is also awareness that in some situations particular issues are raised for children by conflicting rights and notions of responsibility which involve some determination of capacity and protection by adults.

Questions arise as to whether all children can or should be taken seriously – and, if so, at what age? In the child protection arena there are key concerns about safeguarding: about managing the balance between the ethics of care and issues of rights. And there are concerns as to the extent to which the expression of their views might challenge power issues within the family and within the wider community and, if so, how and who will manage this? At the same time there is some ambiguity in policy and practice at government level where, alongside the participation agenda, run practices in health and social care which are directed at greater state control and surveillance of children and families, such as through electronic databases.

There is increasing awareness of the ways in which participation can impact on children as individuals and about the role of professionals in enabling children's effective participation at various levels and in acting upon what they hear. Research evidence of children's participation in a range of arenas suggests that there are positive effects, such as increased self esteem and self confidence. There is also evidence that their views can influence service delivery, such as through Children's Plans, in schools and in policy decisions at local and national levels. However, not all children wish to participate either in individual decisions or in matters of public concern. For them, respect and fairness may be more important than participation *per se*. There is also evidence that, in both organisational and individual decision-making arenas, bureaucratic management structures militate against relationship-based social work which is the cornerstone of empowering practice.

Currently we know little about outcomes, but what information we do have suggests that there may be critical differences where children are participating as a group on more general matters, such as in school councils, and where children are participating in individual situations, such as family meetings, reviews and child protection conferences. In those cases very personal material of a sensitive nature is being shared in a public domain, and skills and great care are needed to ensure their participation is experienced positively. Particular problems arise where, for example, their views on their individual care are in conflict with those of their adult carers or the professionals responsible for their care, such as where parents are separating or where they have been abused. The situation is nuanced and complex and the discourse of politicians, theoreticians and researchers reflects these debates.

This book is an attempt to learn more about the views of children and young people in need on their involvement in decisions about their family life and their care, and to explore some of the transactions in decision-making processes between themselves and the professionals involved. How do children in the social care domain experience and make sense of the participatory processes they have experienced; what responses can or should professionals encourage and make of what they hear, both at individual and at agency levels; what skills and training do the professionals need and what contribution, if any, might participation play in children's wellbeing or wellbecoming when they have been involved in decisions about their life?

The book is divided into two parts. Part I explores the meaning, policy background and context of children's participation. It begins by defining what we mean by participation, sets out the public and private arenas in which children are currently participating and discusses the outcomes to be achieved. Different methods of involving children as individuals or groups are then outlined, from their physical presence, to their representation by other means, including advocacy and consultation. This is followed by an account of the policy background and legal structures in place for enabling children's participation, and an exploration of the theories underpinning participatory practice. Part I ends by exploring the influences of adult attitudes on children's capacity to speak out, the opportunities denied where their social environment is disadvantaged, and the impact of organisational culture and values on the practitioner's ability to work toward participatory practice.

Part II reports on four research studies on the views of children and young people who have received social work help in different environments, and on the responses of their carers and the professional recipients to their views. To embrace as wide a picture as possible, the studies have been chosen to include children of different ages and ability, of different legal status and experiencing different social work interventions and levels of involvement.

The studies presented here include children aged from 6 to 19. The first study describes the views of children aged 6 to 15 who have been included in family group conferences, and where advocacy was available. The second also focuses on children's attendance at decision-making meetings – in this case initial child protection conferences and reviews – where very different issues are raised. The third study explored children's inclusion in the process of electronic social work recording within the Integrated Children's System (ICS) which was being introduced at that time. Based on interviews with children, some of whom had severe disabilities, it illustrates the difficulties in involving children in recording and explores the ongoing issues of privacy, confidentiality and surveillance that are heightened by the use of electronic databases and electronic social care records. The fourth study is somewhat different, and has been selected because it has a wider policy focus. It describes the views of 76 children aged from 6 to 19 on the range of social work help they have received, their understanding of how their views have been fed back to the statutory and voluntary services who have provided it and an account of the responses of the agencies concerned.

In the studies of family group conferences and recording within the ICS, there is an associated commentary on the views of parents and professionals on the children's involvement which illustrates how one affects another. In the one reporting children's views on whether they think their views have influenced agency policy and been taken into account by practitioners, there is also an account of what the statutory and voluntary agencies did as a policy response, both in terms of service delivery and in the larger arena of service planning.

The book concludes by identifying the social work skills illustrated by the research studies that are essential to participatory practice. More broadly, it discusses the ways in which the findings from the research take us forward in our understanding of children's experience of participation in social work interventions, and will it is hoped throw light upon some of the theoretical and organisational issues explored in the earlier chapters.

PART I

The Principles, Policy and Theory Underpinning Practice

CHAPTER 1

What is Participation?

Definitions, Arenas and Outcomes

Definitions

Definitions of what 'participation' means and what it comprises abound.
Kirby *et al.* (2003) describe it as a multi-layered concept which embraces
notions of both process and outcome. The United Nations Committee
on the Rights of the Child 2009 General Comment (No.12) also notes
the process and outcome aspects of participation, and describe how the
term has evolved and is now widely used:

> ...to describe ongoing processes, which include information sharing
> and dialogue between children and adults based on mutual respect,
> and in which children can learn how their views and those of adults
> are taken into account and shape the outcome of such processes. (p.5)

Most commonly the term 'participation' is now used in a broad sense
to cover different types and levels of involvement, to describe a range
of activities taking place in differing circumstances, involving different
types of engagement, and including representation, consultation and
advocacy in widely differing situations.

Participation as taking part

Participation literally means to take part or to share in. So at one level
engagement in a social work intervention by the child or young person
would constitute participation. Service users who do not engage do not
participate. A key social work skill, be it in direct work with children,
or in facilitating their involvement in consultations on the services they
receive, is thus to engage the children and young people so that they
are actively taking part in the process.

Participation as engagement at different levels and in different arenas

Participation takes place in a range of arenas and at different levels, from inclusion in individual decision making, such as in initial child protection conferences and reviews, to involvement in promoting organisational change at local, regional, national and international levels. The levels of participation involved in these arenas vary both in terms of power sharing between children and adults and with regard to the nature and context of the event. In both individual decision making and in organisational change the effectiveness of participation depends both upon the skills of the practitioners supporting them, and also on the culture and organisation of the officiating body. The two are, of course, interdependent.

Participation as achieving different outcomes

Participation is also aimed at achieving different outcomes, from personal empowerment in individual decision making to organisational change. In these diverse situations, as Sinclair, Wilson and Gibbs (2004) point out, the frequency and nature of the participatory activity will vary widely, as will the children and young people involved. For example, effecting the participation of looked-after children in reviews over a number of years is a very different process from involving children in schools in youth forums, and the outcomes to be achieved will also be different. A positive outcome of children's engagement in their reviews could be increased self confidence. The outcome of a child's involvement in a school council could mean that the play space is altered. Unpicking the difference between these participatory transactions and the skills involved is important if we are to understand the dynamics of relationships and organisations that endeavour to promote children's participation, and to explore what gets in the way.

Terminology

Before going any further I should explain that, in this book, I use the terms 'childhood' and 'children' in the way defined by the law – as the period and stage up to age 18, the age of majority. I most commonly talk about 'children's' participation, within which young people are subsumed. However, I am cognisant that there is, as James and James (2004) point out, a danger of using terms such as 'childhood', 'child', 'children' and 'youth' as a collective, since each child/young person is unique and his experiences and conditions hugely various. Government legislation and guidance for working with children is written as if these differences did not exist. They do, and they impact profoundly on practitioners' skills and capacity to involve children in important decisions that affect them. Hopefully the content of this book does address these issues and takes into account and reflects individuality.

Of course, the question of where the boundary with adulthood should be drawn is a tricky one, particularly when considering children's competence to take part in decision making. In determining their competence, three factors are key: age, ability and culture. For example, in considering whether or how to involve a child in a child protection conference, age is significant. On the face of it a 16-year-old may present her views clearly and be less disturbed by what she hears than would a 9-year-old because she is 'more mature'. But this does not take into account her intellectual ability, emotional capacity, family support or background. Neither does it allow for consideration of other abilities, such as mobility or communication – not necessarily linked to age. Nor does it take into account the disadvantages engendered by cultural difference, such as language, gender and custom.

As the story of children's participation progresses throughout the following chapters, these are some of the dilemmas we shall explore.

Participation as taking part

Two of the dictates of social work today are working in partnership and promoting engagement in the process of change through direct work. Involving children in social work interventions is the basis of practice that is effective and empowering – of participatory practice. Indeed, children who have not taken part in the work or felt respected as individuals in their own right are unlikely to engage in the process of change at all.

There are both process and outcome goals of empowerment. Braye and Preston-Shoot (1995, p.126) define empowerment as 'the process of taking control of one's own life', of moving from a position of vulnerability or lacking power toward a position of enhanced power. Individual empowerment is thus about personal development where feelings of self worth, strategies for coping and the idea of choice is instilled. Those processes – and so the outcomes that depend upon them – can only happen where the children take an active role in their social work.

To illustrate some of the ways in which children can be helped to take part in their social work I give an example of an intervention with young children. I have chosen to describe a group work activity with young children in order to demonstrate that:

- the age of the children does not preclude their capacity to take part or be empowered

- a variety of social work methods – in this case group work with puppets – can be employed to achieve engagement

- engaging children in a social work intervention can have as its outcome behavioural change which is empowering.

The example here is of work with young children, aged from 4 to 10, taking part in a parenting programme devised by Webster Stratton (Webster Stratton and Hancock 1998). In this programme, group work is undertaken with young children with behavioural problems, alongside the groups where their parents are being taught parenting skills. Part of the task is to engage both groups in the group work process and to sustain that engagement in order to teach them new skills and strategies for managing their relationship and personal problems. For the children, the objectives are to teach them to manage their feelings, to make friends and to learn social and problem solving skills.

Here a 7-year-old boy describes his learning from the puppet, Tiny Turtle, and the technique he learned to manage his anger:

> 'Stop – go into your shell [Tiny Turtle, the puppet's shell] and do three deep breaths…going along, feeling angry – then, stop, go into your shell and take three deep breaths – feels better when he comes out of his shell…I did that when they were being nasty to me at school. And, yea, I will use it at other times – when I'm an adult. When I get into my car instead of smashing windows you go and ask them to move the car, don't you.' (Bell and Fisher 2004, p.46)

His participation in the work of anger management resulted in an important learning process which should enable him to better manage destructive emotions in the present, with all the positive knock-on and longer-term effects that skill could have for him in terms of his capacity to participate in wider issues and in later life.

Other studies, such as the evaluation of Sure Start by Williams and Churchill (2006) have also identified practices which encourage empowerment in young children, such as self help and mutual support. The effects on the confidence and learned skills of children, even young children, are clear from these studies, and the knock-on benefits in terms of the rights agenda will be explored in more detail later.

However, the picture is not all rosy. There are a number of difficulties in seeking the views of children on personal matters. A recent review on the literature on children's participation and focus group interviews conducted with children by Participation Works (Davey 2010) found that in the most personal decisions that affect them children's views are often not sought. This study covers individual health care, private law proceedings, child protection investigations, the immigration and asylum-seeking process and school exclusion as being areas where children's views are often not sought, and where, if they do appear, they often have little impact.

Turning to taking part in organisational change, participation has become a key target for organisations in both the voluntary and statutory sectors. Investing in Children (see Cairns and Brannen 2005) provides a good example of an organisation that has had some success in engaging children and young people from a range of backgrounds and in promoting their opportunities to contribute to political debate in County Durham. It is a multi-agency partnership, begun a decade ago, that has successfully completed a number of projects to improve public services. The '730+' was one project run by children with diabetes who wanted to improve their treatment. They interviewed hospital staff, organised focus groups and produced a report which resulted in better facilities at the local hospital and greater understanding of their needs.

However, while some specific projects in this initiative achieved success, others, such as better access to community resources, did not impact upon the political agenda. Williamson (2003) conducted an evaluation of Investing in Children and concluded that many of the changes 'require a change in attitudes or in mind sets' (p.29), and that the developments would be difficult to sustain over long periods of time.

Sustaining the enthusiasm and commitment of young people in organisational change is a challenge, especially where the results are unclear to them. In Danso *et al.*'s study (2003), where children within the care system had been given the opportunity to express their views, they felt that they were not taken into account. Danso suggests there is 'consultation fatigue', and reports 'What's the point?' responses from children when asked if they want to take part in yet another consultation exercise. A particular problem was that the deadlines for completing projects and tasks were too tight, resulting in disillusionment all round.

Lightfoot and Sloper (2003) also found that disillusionment sets in quickly if the ideas of the young people are not implemented, or they feel that their ideas are fed back to adults rather than to them (a process common with children with disabilities) and they sense the process was tokenistic. Linked to this is that they needed evidence that any participatory processes they had been involved in had some positive outcomes. While anecdotal evidence is relatively easy to come by, rigorous evaluations were not often demonstrated.

So, while taking part is an essential starting point for children's participation, and the values, skills and commitment of adults to engagement are similar whatever the arena, openness, honesty and clear feedback about results and outcomes is necessary to ensure the children do not end up thinking their voices were sought but not heard, and that the process was tokenistic.

Participation at different levels

Levels of active engagement can helpfully be seen in terms of the degrees of power sharing between adults and children (Shier 2001). The earliest conceptualisation of these aspects of power was delineated by Arnstein in 1969. In describing planning processes in the United States, she constructed a ladder of participation which delineated three levels of power sharing, from degrees of tokenism to degrees of citizen power.

- *Level 1 – Manipulation and tokenism*: On the lowest rungs were manipulation and tokenism – both non-participant, the aim being to cure or educate the participants. The response of young people in the UK to Anti-Social Behaviour Orders (ASBOs) provides a good example of how a policy intended to gain young people's engagement in change, to 'cure' their bad behaviour, has been experienced as tokenistic, and has been unsuccessful in achieving either their co-operation or a change in their behaviour (see Garrett 2007).

- *Level 2 – Informing, consulting and placation:* At the second level, informing, consulting and placation are seen as legitimate steps. Providing information, for example in relation to how an assessment will be carried out, is an essential beginning to engaging young people in the social work process from assessment to review. And information and feedback about what has happened are key aspects of motivation and engagement. Children's participation at all levels depends upon the information that is made available to them at the outset, as well as whether their views are taken into account as an outcome.

    Consultation is also a key part of gaining the views of children, for example about their wishes in cases of parental contact. However, those processes can also involve degrees of tokenism. If a child is consulted but her views not taken into account the process is tokenistic and can result in a loss of trust between the practitioner and the child. Placation, also, can be tokenistic – for example, where selected 'worthies' are voted onto committees, or where, in individual work, children are assured that 'everything will be all right', when this cannot be guaranteed.

- *Level 3 – Partnership to citizen control:* Finally the last three rungs of Arnstein's ladder comprise degrees of citizen power which include partnership. Partnership comprises a redistribution of power – from delegated power through to citizen control. The redistribution of power is central to the process.

    > Participation without redistribution of power is an empty and frustrating process for the powerless. It allows the power holders to claim that all sides were considered but makes it possible for only some of these sides to benefit. (Arnstein 1969, p.216)

Arnstein did not, of course, have children and young people at the centre of her conceptualisation of power sharing. As we have already indicated, there are particular issues relating to adults' ability to share power with children, and *vice versa*, which have more recently become central to the consideration of children's participation. However, despite the fact that other writers have subsequently modified or adapted Arnstein's ladder to reflect a process rather than a hierarchical view, all models do contain essentially the same components and are applicable to children and young people.

In considering social workers working in partnership with families in child protection Thoburn (1995) reduced the levels of partnership to three: information provision, consultation and active participation. At this time, following the publication of *The Challenge of Partnership in Child Protection* (Department of Health 1995) which outlined 15 principles for working in partnership with children and families, research commonly focused on unpicking social work practice to analyse what, within the client–worker relationship, promoted the empowerment of clients. Bell (1995) analysed the transactions between professionals and 83 families involved in initial child protection conferences; Marsh and Fisher (1992) explored the relationship between social workers and service users in Bradford. While the detail of the analysis focused on social work practice – for example, the need for explicit consent and the use of negotiated agreement between client and worker – the conclusions of Marsh and Fisher were broader based in turning the focus from social workers' practice skills onto organisational issues, in particular culture.

> Users can play a key role in informing the development of policy and practice…but that belief in the value of partnership contrasts with the low recognition of users' views. Staff may resist change towards participation, openness and information because they 'do this already'. (Marsh and Fisher 1992, p.4)

Interest in refining conceptualisations of participation and partnership continued. Hart's (1997) 'ladder of participation' also comprises eight rungs, each rung describing different aspects of power sharing from non-participation – manipulation and tokenism – to degrees of participation. The bottom three rungs continue to comprise manipulation, decoration (for example, where children wear T-shirts promoting a cause), and tokenism, where children's views are heard but not acted upon (for example in some court proceedings). The remaining five rungs all include some genuine participation, up to the top rung where children initiate processes and share decisions with adults. These are situations where 'children initiate their own project' and where 'they should be allowed to direct and manage the project' (Hart 1997, p.45).

Hart's ladder is thus very similar to Arnstein's although the discourse – reflecting the increasing concerns about children's rights and children's disempowerment – involves children as well as adults. Again, the structure is hierarchical and based on power, although Hart differs somewhat in where he draws the line between non-participation and degrees of participation. On Hart's ladder the lowest three rungs are all non-participant.

Following this, the validity of the hierarchical concept of the ladder or pyramid, with the objective of striving for the top rung, was further questioned. In New Zealand Treseder (1997) developed a circular model to demonstrate how children and young people can be involved to varying degrees in project decision making (see Figure 1.1). This model recognises that in certain arenas, such as schools and councils, children's involvement will never result in children and young people completely controlling the decision that is made although they have contributed to it.

Treseder's circular model takes into account the wide range of activities in which children are participating and the context in which decisions are made. His definition continues to be used. Participation Works (Davey 2010, p.7) base their review of children's participation in home, family and school on an adaptation of his definition: 'Participation is a process where someone influences decisions about their lives and this leads to change.'

An interesting dimension here is the association of participation with the 'successful' outcomes of influence and change, since this implies that, if change does not happen the process has not been participatory. Certainly, as will become clear when we look at the research on children's experiences, the relationship between process and outcome is not straightforward. Children can feel they have participated, as they do in some of the family group conferences described in Chapter 6, even if the outcome is not what they hoped for. The outcome the child is endeavouring to achieve may be different from the outcome the parent or social worker is aiming toward. So, although the outcome in terms of the decision made will be determined differently in terms of 'success' by the actors involved, the process can be empowering for the children because they have felt included.

Table 1.1 Levels of partnership with service users

Partnership process	Arnstein (1969)	Hart (1992)	Thoburn, Lewis and Shemmings (1995)	Shier (2001)
Higher level of partnership	Citizen control	Child-initiated, shared decisions with adults	Delegated power Involvement in service design	Children share power and responsibility in the decision making
	Delegated power	Child-initiated and directed		
	Partnership	Adult-initiated, shared decisions with adults	Partnership participation	Children are involved in decision-making processes
	Placation	Consulted and informed	Involvement consultation	Children's views are taken into account
	Consultation	Assigned but informed	Keeping fully informed	Children are supported in expressing their views
		Tokenism		Children are listened to
Lower level of partnership	Therapy	Decoration	Placation	
	Manipulation	Manipulation	Manipulation	

Source: adapted from Sinclair and Franklin (2000)

It is now more generally accepted that different levels of involvement and different mechanisms will be appropriate for different tasks and will also depend upon the outcomes to be achieved. Shier (2001) adapts the ladder to enable practitioners to determine which of five levels of participation is best, from listening through to sharing power. He also advocates organisations to think in terms of 'openings, opportunities and obligations'.

Williams (2005) further develops the process view by stressing that the process is not a hierarchy where the 'aim' is to reach the top of the ladder. Kirby's model (Kirby *et al.* 2003) is also circular, non-hierarchical and process based (see Figure 1.2).

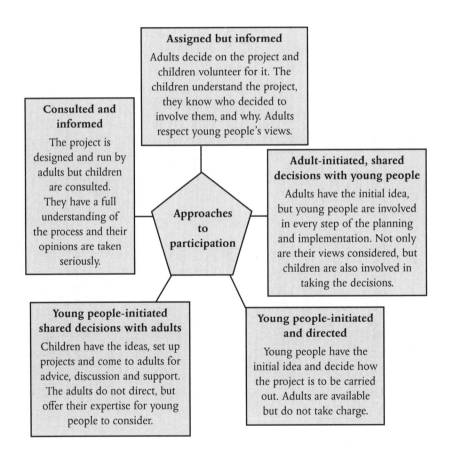

Figure 1.1 Approaches to participation (Treseder 1997)

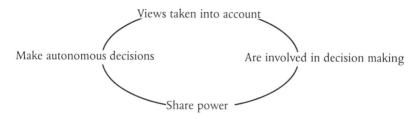

Figure 1.2 Kirby's model of participation (Cutler 2003)

Certainly, this shift in the conceptualisation of process, from Arnstein's steps on the ladder to Treseder, Kirby and Williams' notions of circularity, does allow us to see children's participation in both individual decision making and in organisational issues as progressive and nuanced. While some engagements may be experienced by a child as tokenistic, others may be fruitful, depending upon a wide range of factors. For example, the Participation Works (Davey 2010) survey of organisations and participation workers suggests that the age of the children was critical to their engagement. Secondary-school-aged children were more likely to be involved in decision making than primary-school-aged children. For example, children at Park View secondary school in Tottenham elect their own year representatives to take their views to the youth forum where decisions about catering, safety in school and saving for charities is discussed. From a girl in Year 8:

> 'I'd like to make the school a happier and safer place and make sure everyone has a say.' (Bell 2011)

Participation in different arenas

Clearly, the outcomes to be achieved by children and young people's participation vary according to the arena in which the participation is happening. Theoreticians differ in their definitions of arena. Sinclair and Franklin (2000) separate private (within the family or between individuals) and public (service) arenas, but make a further distinction between decisions relating to an individual, and those relating to a group.

Kirby *et al.* (2003) delineate participation as taking place in three arenas:

- where individual decisions are being taken about children's own lives
- where services for or used by children are being delivered locally
- where national policies are being developed or evaluated.

Wright *et al.* (2006, p.9) reduce this to two by collapsing the latter two together into 'collective involvement in matters that affect them', be they local or national services or policies.

A further way of defining arenas has been suggested by Moss (2002), who conceives public provisions as 'children's spaces'. Spaces can be social, such as relationships, cultural, such as values and rights, and discursive, such as dialogue or deliberation. One of the key points illustrated by the research studies described later in this book, is the importance of the 'social space' of relationship in facilitating children's participation in decision making. Time and again, and in a variety of situations, such as in assessments and in leaving care, it is the children's relationship with their social worker that enables them to engage and take part. At an organisational level also, for example in school councils, the culture and dialogue of the interaction also contribute to the child having a voice which is heard.

Hill *et al.* (2004) suggest that the concept of children's spaces alters ways of thinking about the relationship between professional and service users, so that both groups contain expertise and knowledge while the professionals are the facilitators. As we know from serious case reviews (see Brandon *et al.* 2008) the information children can provide to professionals can be essential to safe decision making. Again, the idea of process and inclusion is central to this conceptualisation of arenas and relationships, while the acknowledgment that all stakeholders bring expertise highlights a positive feature: that children also hold power although it may be expressed and experienced as different from adults.

These concepts convey different emphases in thinking about the connections between context, process and arena. Whatever the discourse, there is agreement that the participatory activities in which children and young people are involved occupy different spaces – and range from service planning and service development to situations where children may be involved as subjects in their own right.

Participation as achieving different outcomes

Turning to the outcomes to be achieved in these varied arenas, there is some common ground that relates to process. Children's engagement in both individual decision-making arenas and in organisational change, for example, shares features such as taking part and being committed. From another pupil at Park View School:

> 'School is not just about what my school and teachers can do for me, it's also about what I can do for my school.' (Bell 2011)

The capacity to present views clearly and to be heard is also important to achieve change, irrespective of the arena or the purpose of the enterprise. However, there are also differences in the intended outcomes.

In the case of individual decision-making arenas the outcome to be achieved is a personal one, often involving key decisions about where the child can live, who he or she can have contact with…and so on. The family group and the child are the most affected by the decision. In the case of organisational change, on the other hand, the objectives are to bring about change outside of self, that is, with the organisation or policy. The process of participation will therefore also include some different aspects, such as consulting others in the group and presenting views effectively to a number of audiences. This girl from Park View School, representing Year 9, puts this succinctly:

> 'Even though this is a leadership role, I don't want to be seen as a leader. I would like to be seen as a representative.' (Bell 2011)

And in the arenas of local services and national policies the mechanisms, skills, tasks and opportunities for being involved also differ. The Who Cares? Trust (1998), for example, has resources, contacts and experience of meeting with ministers at national level which are not available to local groups involved in community initiatives – and their purposes may differ.

Despite the different goals of the participatory practice and the arena in which it takes place, there is evidence that positive outcomes are achieved by children's participation, both in personal and in organisational domains. Although children's estimation of the services they receive varies, a consistent finding is that they do value involvement in decisions which concern them, and that they are therefore more likely to maintain engagement which underpins change (Sinclair, Wilson and Gibbs 2001). All social workers and social work programmes, with all ages of children and young people, should therefore provide evidence that they engage children and their carers in the change process. Positive involvement and engagement underpin participatory practice, irrespective of the arena in which it takes place.

In relation to personal empowerment, the benefits for children of participation at both individual and organisational levels include learning new skills, such as presentation and negotiation, as well as increased self confidence and a stronger sense of self worth. This can happen at an individual level, in meetings and reviews, for example, as well as at an organisational level, in forums, councils, etc. The research carried out by Participation Works (Davey 2010) showed that children developed confidence and public speaking skills as a result of being a member of a school council or youth forum. They had opportunities 'to negotiate and think through problems from different angles and to use their own initiative' (p.11). Mostly these decisions were around what food they wanted rather than deciding how school budgets should be spent.

There is evidence that enhanced self esteem and greater self confidence are built upon children's experiences that their views are valued. Research studies (Bell and Fisher 2004; Grimshaw and McGuire 1998) demonstrate that, where children are engaged in the therapeutic social work process, the objectives, for example, to teach new skills and strategies, are achieved. In some cases practitioners work specifically with a child to teach them how to manage their anger, as described previously in the account of the Webster Stratton children's groups earlier in this chapter. In others the development of new skills can result from the self worth experienced as a result of the positive relationship and care devoted by the practitioner who can become the child's 'secondary attachment' figure (see Bell 2002; Holland 2010). Chapter 7 describes the importance of the role practitioners can play as a secondary attachment figure in child protection investigations.

However, before outlining some specific outcomes of personal skill development as a result of participatory practice, a note of caution. From the child's perspective an outcome could be that they feel better, have a positive attitude, feel respected, and so on. Difficult to measure! From the agency's perspective a positive outcome could be that more children have attended reviews or child protection conferences whereas, in fact, representation by other means might have been the child's preference and more effective. In practice, the young person may have experienced their review as a waste of time and boring (Sinclair 1998) or the young person may find that the school policy on bullying does not reflect the views she carefully presented in the school council – the process therefore may feel tokenistic and not worth the time and effort. Similarly, the child's contribution to a social work record could be monitored, but would not necessarily provide evidence that the child had felt included, nor would it portray the quality of that transaction, nor of its effect on future events. This could really only be rated by the child and by longitudinal research.

Positive outcomes: personal
PARTNERSHIP AND NEGOTIATION SKILLS

Strategies learned in participatory practice provide excellent models of transaction for the children involved. For example, in working toward partnership in the social work relationship, children are required to give their explicit consent to the involvement, where the contract of the engagement is negotiated and what it comprises (Corden and Preston-Shoot 1987; Marsh and Fisher 1992). This can give a level of influence and an element of choice about the provision offered which can help young service users to understand their own wants and needs, as well as to learn and practise some of the processes of negotiating and prioritising. For example, a written contract, signed by the child, may include an agreement about times of meeting, what will be discussed and what it is hoped to achieve. Where social workers have worked toward such a contract, or helped children to include it in their records, it is far more likely that they will engage and co-operate. And these skills will stand them in good stead in future transactions, be they personal or business.

FEELINGS OF SELF WORTH AND BETTER BEHAVIOUR

Where young people have been engaged constructively in their social work or in consulting on policy issues, this also carries with it benefits which will further their capacity to participate in wider issues. Developing confidence and feelings of self worth can enable them to deal with personal and family problems more constructively. Chapter 7 describes children's experiences of child protection investigations. This quote from a 9-year-old boy illustrates how the gain in his self confidence meant his behaviour substantially improved:

'Since the ICPC things have got better because I've been going out and coming in at proper times and going to bed when I'm told. I'm fine now – my confidence has improved…speak better, sleep better… at school things are better because I used to fight nearly everyday – but at this school I'm good.'

Such positive experiences can also empower children to become involved in issues outside the family, such as in community initiatives or school councils.

VOICE AND CHOICE

Starkey (2003) introduces the notion of voice – that is, having a say in service provision – as a way of enabling young service users to be aware of choices, to exercise choice and to have the opportunity to voice dissatisfaction. This quote is from a 15-year-old girl who had been using drugs, and was talking about how her participation in a family group conference really helped her, as reported in Chapter 6:

'…I had the choice whether I wanted to go [to the drug scheme] or not and all the family around me decided whether it was a good idea, and whether it was good for me. I think it was me that made the decisions really. So that's good, because I've never been able to do that before, I've just had social workers just making decisions for me, you know, without even consulting me, so that was really *brilliant*, because you get to decide yourself.'

It also provides a good example of what Lister (2005) conceptualises as 'agency' as it describes the process of acquiring the confidence to act in a purposeful, autonomous way, and to positively experience being taken seriously.

IDENTITY AND SELF ESTEEM

Having an awareness of agency contributes to identity and self esteem and is, in turn, influenced by them. So, it is important that professional practices enable opportunities for agency to be effected. Such processes provide important learning which can then be extended to the wider arena. Looked-after children who have good experience of assessments, conferences and reviews are well placed to transfer their learning to organisational issues.

The involvement of looked-after young people in the Who Cares? Trust can be seen as a product of their positive experience of and skills gained in a social work intervention. In 2009, the trust ran a project called Building Futures, where young people took part in an intensive three-day course to build confidence and prepare for the workplace before embarking on a fortnight's placement. The overall aim of the project was to provide care leavers with work experience opportunities, which would enable them to gain valuable skills and experience to enhance their employment opportunities.

BETTER DECISIONS

Participation can lead to more accurate, relevant decisions which are better informed and therefore more likely to be implemented. The importance of listening to what the child has to say in situations of child protection or domestic violence can not be over-stressed, as child abuse inquiries have many times brought home. And better decision making in agencies can also be a result of listening to children's experiences of service delivery.

Positive outcomes: service delivery, policy and training

ENHANCED SKILLS

In working toward organisational or policy change and in youth forums and councils, young people have developed skills of communication and presentation – verbally, in writing reports and in their use of technology. For example, in talking to a group of trainee social workers about her experience in care, Marie produced a brilliant PowerPoint presentation, some small group exercises for the trainees to work on and a role play exercise. Such experience and skills will stand her in good stead in an employment capacity.

BETTER SERVICES

At an organisational level, the benefits are that services become more responsive to the needs of children and young people, and more accessible and efficient as they are providing a more effective service. The study described in Chapter 9 illustrates a number of ways in which the local authority took on board the views of the children. For example, the complaints procedure for young people was revised following consultation with a group of young people who had complained. As a result, the complaints officer was upgraded to the senior management group and a hotline to the assistant director was set up. This ensured that complaints were taken beyond the individual level and that the feedback was also given to the Area Child Protection Committee and to team managers. Clear time scales and the use of advocates from a voluntary agency ensured that the young person knew what had happened as a result of their complaints.

CONTRIBUTIONS TO OTHER ORGANISATIONS, SUCH AS CHARITIES AND RESEARCH

The value of listening to the views of children has been demonstrated by the National Youth Agency, which maintains a database on participation. Their report (2008) says that 80 per cent of statutory and voluntary sector organisations currently involve young people in decision making. Many children's charities include an advisory group of young people.

And it is now considered good research practice to have a steering and/or consultation group led by or involving young people. An example of this is described in the Introduction to Part II, where a young people's group worked together with the researcher to identify what research questions about the Integrated Children's System might engage the young service users as well as the most opportune environment for carrying out the research.

INPUT TO RESOURCES AND TRAINING

Young people, especially those who are looked after, are increasingly being involved in information distribution and advertising, and in training. Participation Works is a UK organisation set up to provide 'online access to the world of children and young people's participation', including access to information and resources on, for example, rights and governance. Young people aged 16–19 are approved as trainers, and help to run workshops on Hear by Right (HBR), a tool designed to enable organisations to map and develop the extent of young people's participation within their organisation.

Hear by Right comprises a set of standards for the active involvement of children and young people. The National Youth Agency (NYA) based the standards on the 'Seven S' framework, which forms a practical evidence-based model of how to achieve change in organisations and is thought to promote a shared dialogue between service providers and their users. The framework comprises:

- shared values
- strategies

- structures
- systems
- staff
- skills and knowledge
- style of leadership.

The NYA have a brief to work with Children's Trusts to embed Hear by Right, and many organisations, such as West Kent Housing and Cheshire Youth Groups, are using the tools created to improve their services. Young people are also involved in the delivery of training courses such as Ready Steady Change, a course introducing agencies to tools and materials to increase young people's effective participation in decision making; and to the consultancy package, Building a Culture of Participation. Investing in Children, described earlier, also has a programme of staff development training which it delivers to partners and organisations. The training is delivered by two adults and two young people, its overall purpose being to create a greater understanding of the issues faced by children and young people in society.

LILAC is an organisation, initiated by A National Voice (an organisation run by young people in care and care leavers), that recruits and trains young people in care to inspect local authority children's services. The inspections are based on standards that the young people themselves have set, and the evaluation of pilot projects that they have carried out has demonstrated that they are able to open up and share truths with experienced inspectors (see www.fostering.net).

INFLUENCE ON NATIONAL AND INTERNATIONAL POLICIES

At national level different groups of young people have taken on responsibility for influencing political decision making and debate. The Children's Rights Alliance, for example, seeks to promote the rights of children and young people and is proactive in encouraging young people to participate in their projects. The Alliance has appointed young people as full trustees on its Board of Management, and have recently taken part in England's 'Get ready for Geneva' project, which campaigns for children's rights in England to be respected and better protected. They are also involved in international debate. Through the Geneva project they form part of the United Nations' reporting process for the Convention on the Rights of the Child. Also at an international level, the Who Cares? Trust is involved with the rights of young people in Zimbabwe.

Evaluating outcomes

However, although we can list a number of positive outcomes of children's participation in organisational arenas, researchers do continue to evidence that, even when structures to promote participation have been put in place and models developed, there are continuing problems in evaluating outcomes. Wade (2003) suggest that there are two main questions organisations need to ask themselves: is there evidence that children and young people have been actively listened to, and is there evidence of change as a result?

There is evidence that local authorities do not formally evaluate the impact of their initiatives. Oldfield and Fowler (2004) found limited use of monitoring and formal evaluation procedures in both the voluntary and statutory sectors. Franklin and Sloper (2004) also found that participation was fragile and often rested on a few individuals within an organisation. Where key staff had a wider remit this aspect was not always prioritised. There was a need for dedicated funding, not always available now nor in the longer term. And while there are requirements on local authorities and the courts to progress children's participation, there are no formal mechanisms in place for evaluating outcomes.

In relation to children with disabilities, Franklin and Sloper found that more than half of the social service departments they researched could not indicate change resulting from the involvement of young people. Where change had occurred it referred to changes in the activities offered, rather than at a decision-making level.

Kirby et al. (2003) suggest four reasons why organisations fail to evidence outcomes:

- They lack confidence, being at an early stage in the process.
- They focus on monitoring rather than on outcomes (so they describe what they've done rather than what has changed).
- They have difficulty in evidencing possible outcomes, such as increased self esteem.
- They find it difficult to attribute change to the young people's participation.

However, the problem does seem more endemic than Kirby thought. The 2010 report by Participation Works identifies the same three key barriers to involving children.

> The first was the low number of organisations who were proactively measuring the impact...the second and third...concerned the need for better promotion of the benefits...and...the need for better senior management commitment to children's participation. (Davey 2010, p.12)

Overall, then, it seems outputs, rather than outcomes, are being evidenced. The Social Care Institute for Excellence's review of service user participation (Carr 2004) also found little evidence of achieved outcomes. The worry is that the uncertainty about how to involve children in ways that bring about active change, including managing organisational change, is continuing. Some of these issues are explored in detail in Chapter 9 which reports on a study in one local authority of the structures in place to collect and respond to children's views.

This chapter has explored what participation means, discussed evolving definitions of the use of the term and looked at the outcomes that can be achieved in the different arenas in which children's participation takes place. There are a number of ways in which children's views can be elicited and represented, and these will be discussed in the next chapter.

CHAPTER 2

What is Participation?

Different Methods

Having looked at what participation comprises and at some of the outcomes of children's participation in both individual and organisational decision-making arenas, we turn now to consider the best means of carrying it out. The participation of children and young people can be effected by differing methods. The choice of method will depend on a range of factors: the age and ability of the child, the resources available and the arena in which the participation is taking place.

Methods of involving children and effecting their participation vary from establishing their physical presence – singly in individual decision making or in groups in political and organisational change – to their representation by different means, such as through written scripts and reports, pictures and drawings or by audio-tape, video or computers. The use of advocates has extended as advocacy services have been developed, in particular by voluntary services. Where there are language and/or communication difficulties interpreters or experts need to be trained and available to present the views of the children and to translate back to them what is going on. Finally, consultation is also a method of communicating views which is essential to participatory practice, especially at an organisational level, though consultation is more likely to comprise information sharing and to be project based.

The child's presence

In individual decision-making arenas, such as in assessments or reviews, as well as in consultations and involvement in organisations, the physical presence of the child or group concerned should be considered in the first instance. This can be important in terms of information sharing so that the child can see, hear and contribute to what is going on and so that others can see, hear and respond to him. It will also give an important message to the child about inclusion.

Being present may enable the child to take part in the decision-making process and to know what decisions are made. And the child may feel he has been heard and has been influential. This quote from a 13-year-old girl (see Chapter 7) who had been sexually abused by her father, and attended a child protection conference, portrays a sense of her feeling included:

> 'I went to the first part of the conference – it was OK. They were finding things out and what I thought…they told me what had been decided – to sort out school, health and so on. I said I thought it would be best to go into care.'

The role and skills of the social worker and other professionals involved can be essential in terms of preparation and management, and in ensuring that the experience is positive for both the child and for other family members or the professionals involved. The child needs to know and trust the social worker. The location and timing should be appropriate for the child. And careful preparation before the meeting and sensitive management by the chairperson all help to ensure the child's experience will be positive.

However, in some cases the child's physical presence may not be appropriate. As already indicated, the child's age, ability or emotional state might mean they are unable to speak for themselves, or that they could be harmed by what they hear and see. Some children do not want to be present. Research (see Bell 1999c) also suggests that, if the child is present, professionals may withhold important information that they fear could harm the child. In child protection meetings, where all essential information needs to be shared in the multi-disciplinary team, the consequences of silence can be dangerous. In these cases other means of representing the views of the child need to be in place.

Representing the views of the child

Where children's physical presence is inappropriate, their views need to be presented by other means.

Scripts, drawings, videos, symbols boards, etc.

In the individual decision-making arena, such as in meetings, reviews and in court, the child's views can be presented by written statements, including on computers, worked on with the social worker before a meeting. Audio or video recordings could also be prepared. With younger children drawings could be shown and interpreted. For children with disabilities there are some specialist facilities to aid communication. Talking Mats, for example, is an exercise which provides a set of question-based 'mats' with symbols attached. The children are asked questions, such as 'Are you happy at school?' and invited to choose a symbol that matches their feelings. A symbols board – or talking mat – is then created which enables communication via signing, pointing or talking to be developed. Although to date there is little information on their use, and few practitioners are trained in using them (Mitchell *et al.* 2009), symbols boards can be created by practitioners and used to make the child's views known to the meeting.

Intermediaries

Turning to representation by intermediaries, the example of Children's Guardians, who represent the views of the child in court, illustrates both the strengths and difficulties of this method. Children's Guardians need to have spent considerable time before the hearing getting to know children and building up trust. They may use play, materials and exercises to enable children to tell them what they want the court to hear. Exercises such as 'Draw my Family' help children to describe their family, particularly in terms of feelings. 'Helping Hand' is an exercise to help children identify who they trust, who they want to talk to when they are happy and when they are worried, by drawing round their hand and decorating it. One finger represents a safe person, another one who is dangerous – and so on (Turning Points Resource Pack, NSPCC and Chailey Heritage 2006). With older children a number of tools are now available for practitioners to use in talking to them. My Turn to Talk (National Children's Bureau 2005) is a guide to help young people aged over 12 who are in care to 'have a say' about how they are looked after in relation to their education, future plans, reviews and care.

Having elicited the child's views through play or exercises, as well as through talking to them, the Guardian is then able to present them to the court. However, this role – as a representative – is different from both advocacy and social work roles since the Guardian has duties to fulfil which may counter ones associated with those roles. First, the Guardian has a duty to present his professional judgement on what is in the child's best interests, which may not be what the child has said she wants. For example, the child might want contact with a parent who the Guardian has assessed as abusive and unsafe – and so recommends against contact arrangements being set up. Second, he has a duty to comment critically on the social worker's recommendation, which could be different from his own.

In so far as children's participation is concerned, a number of conflicts abound in both the Guardian's and the social worker's role in court. Bilson and White (2005) see this conflict as being inherent in Articles 3 and 12 of the UNCRC, which give two imperatives which may be compatible but which may also conflict. Article 3 states that 'the best interests of the child shall be a primary consideration'; Article 12, that 'the views of the child should be given due weight in accordance with the age and maturity of the child'. The weight that is attached to these imperatives affects the way that approaches to addressing children's needs for representation are addressed, and the judgements reflect the roles of the professionals concerned rather than the child's views. It may therefore be more accurate to describe the Guardian's role as representation, rather than advocacy.

Elected representatives

Turning to children's participation in the organisational arena, particularly where children are participating in groups, there are somewhat different problems of representation. Sinclair *et al.* (2004) ask the question: are children being asked to draw on their own personal experiences or do we expect or enable them to speak on behalf of larger groups of children? A linked concern, also identified by Arnstein (1969), is the possibility of the emergence of 'professional children', that is, children who organisations feel safe including, but who may, by definition, not rock the boat. Who are they representing, and might conflict and difference be suppressed?

Representation is problematic where young people are participating in big decision-making arenas. Middleton (2006), in describing the involvement of young people in the national Youth Matters conference, points out that 'out of numerous presentations throughout the day, just four young people were asked to speak, three of whom were in the 13–19 range' (p.6). Questions arise about whether only some children are being targeted; whether they represent what may often be diverse interests; and whether they can or should be held accountable for actions taken on their advice.

The same dynamic has been reported by researchers. In conducting their research on the participation of children with disabilities, Franklin and Sloper (2009) suggest it is likely that the children who are approached are those who are easiest to reach, are most confident and articulate, and most able to communicate. Their views therefore get represented in the research. Issues of ability to communicate, the tools that are used, and the language of the child are pertinent in relation to whose views actually get communicated or heard.

The National Youth Advocacy Service (2009) provides another example of children being excluded because of their lack of capacity to participate. They surveyed the views of young people in residential special schools, and found that many were unable to communicate effectively – and so their views were not included in the survey.

Further, the style and methods used to promote participation within an organisation can have an effect on whether or not young people engage with them. Bureaucracy, generally, is off-putting. Starkey (2003) draws attention to the disempowering effects of, for example, the use of unfamiliar jargon, and the attitude that 'professionals know best'. Managing the tension between using expertise effectively, and it being experienced as off-putting requires professional awareness and skill. Forums, as a method of encouraging participation, were the least popular with the young people in their study. They were seen as lacking purpose, were not accountable and were not integrated into the organisations' feedback structures.

Participation by advocacy

In the arena of individual decision making the use of an advocate might be the most effective way of ensuring the child's voice is heard. Meetings, complaints and entitlement issues provide some good examples of where advocacy could be a more appropriate means of representation than the child's physical presence or the use of written material. Indeed, a number of authorities use advocates in social work meetings and reviews.

In 2002 the national advocacy standards were published: the Adoption and Children Act (2002) requires all local authorities to provide local advocacy services for children. Most advocacy services were established between 1996 and 2000, and most are delivered by national children's voluntary organisations, such as the Children's Society, or by local children's rights services. Advocacy services for looked-after children have increased rapidly following Utting's (1997) recognition of the important role of advocacy in protecting this vulnerable group, and most authorities have either made arrangements for advocates to be available, or have Children's Rights Officers who perform that function.

The different models in use include advocacy services commissioned from independent organisations, the Independent Visitor Service, and spot purchasing from such organisations as the National Youth Advocacy Service. Children's advocacy services have therefore been developed largely around the needs of looked-after young people, some for disabled children, some for children making complaints – but few are routinely available to those involved in social work procedures. Despite the recommendations of the National Minimum Standards for Children's Homes (Department of Health 2002b) only a small number have Independent Visitors for looked-after young people who have no contact with their families. A study by Ofsted (2008) found that one in four children receiving social care did not know what an advocate was, and a further 16 per cent did not know how to access one.

Defining advocacy is important because there are differences in how it is understood. Advocacy comprises a range of activities including advocating the young person's view as well as addressing rights issues. Individual advocacy focuses on the particular issue at hand and enables young people to voice their concerns. Advocates also deal with general rights issues beyond the particular context. In contrast, social workers focus on the best interests of the child, and work collaboratively with other professionals. Although *Care Matters* (DCSFY 2006) uses the terms 'mentor', 'independent visitor' and 'advocate' interchangeably, the role of mentors and Independent Visitors is not necessarily to address their problems, whereas the role of advocates is.

Oliver, Knight and Candappa (2006) describe the dominant understanding among advocates as combining 'elements of representation, support, empowerment, and protection of rights' (p.2). In their study, the advocates defined their role as being to 'speak up' on behalf of children, enabling them to 'have a voice', or to 'put their views across', rather than as being to ensure young people had access to services. In so far as the young people and their parents or carers were concerned, there was some initial confusion about the meaning of advocacy, although experiences were generally positive. Advocates were described as being supportive and 'on my side', and as providing information and rebalancing power in decision-making arenas. They were also seen as being more available and accessible, and the young people valued their independence. Social care professionals, while seeing their roles as complementary, were also more equivocal in their definitions. They lacked awareness of what the advocates actually did or they saw their role as being potentially confrontational.

In Oliver *et al.*'s survey, most of the young people who contacted advocacy services did so to get help with placement issues. Others wanted help with bullying, harassment and with contact with family and friends. Barnes (2007) studied four children's rights services to identify the main advocacy services received. These comprised individual advocacy about care and entitlements, advocacy at review meetings and help with complaints. In this study, the young people had difficulty understanding the role of advocates, which they were unable to distinguish from other care workers. They did comment, however, that the practice of advocates differed with respect to confidentiality and the qualities of respect. The main difficulties were in making complaints against their care because they feared repercussions as a result of their disclosure. And they needed training in assertiveness skills.

There are a number of issues that the role of children's advocacy raises. As suggested above, one of the main difficulties in understanding the advocacy role is in distinguishing its difference from the role of other care professionals. In Oliver *et al.*'s study, most respondents compared advocates with social workers and complaints officers. The advocates said the difference was that they presented the child's wishes, whereas other care professionals prioritised their view of the child's best interests.

This highlights the difficulty within advocacy of managing conflicting interests. Children's views are situated alongside the views of other stakeholders and will often represent only one of several sets of voices. The question arises: how are children's views to be weighted alongside these several perspectives? In Bilson and White's study (2005) the professionals thought that in some cases advocates risked undermining parents in decision making, while in others advocates needed to be more on the child's side. Advocates have the problem of whether or not to take context into account, to make judgements – or merely to repeat a young person's wishes.

Another issue in advocacy is the degree to which the processes and objectives are child led. While there is agreement in principle that being child led is a primary objective of advocacy, the evidence from practice suggests that children do not always lead the process. In the studies described above, advocates struggled with taking into account the child's age and maturity, and with being sure they had fully understood the child's wishes. They also lacked the range of communication skills required with, in particular, disabled children.

Does advocacy help or make any difference to outcomes? In Oliver *et al.*'s (2006) study, respondents rated 35 per cent of decisions as being in the young person's favour, for example enhancing care packages. There was a widely held view that advocacy was empowering to children, enhancing their self esteem, and the majority of young people reported a high level of satisfaction with their experience. In some cases policies had been changed, such as improvements in the conduct of review meetings and simpler procedures for overnight stays although bureaucratic procedures and professional attitudes were seen as continuing to create resistance to change. Dalrymple (2005) points out that in court advocacy can lead to greater participation of children, although the issues of their vulnerability cannot be ignored.

Participation by consultation

Hill *et al.* (2004) point out that the precise links between participation and consultation are complex and that the terms are often used interchangeably. He suggests that while participation means the direct involvement of children in decision making, consultation is about seeking views. However, as we have seen, the term 'direct involvement' is itself ambiguous, carrying with it the possibility of advocacy and representation. Equally, consultation can be direct or indirect, and effective or not.

Vis and Thomas (2009) also make a useful distinction between consultation and participation. In their research in Norway, 16 case managers reported consulting with children in 46.5 per cent of the 43 cases they were involved with. However, they did not distinguish between planned consultations for a specific purpose, such as to investigate what happened, and casual conversation on a more general level. The point is that consulting with children and ensuring their participation are different – and one does not necessarily lead to another. They suggest that participation has to be facilitated as a process and not as a one-off event. And that this is a key feature which distinguishes it from consultation.

Like advocacy, consultation could achieve a wider and more informed response – certainly in the arena of political matters – than physical presence or advocacy. The arenas in which children are now consulted are increasing. Middleton (2006) reports successful results of young people's consultation, such as a new bus service for young people in Dorset and setting up a youth club in Cumbria. Children and Young Persons Plans need to be based on consultation exercises, and some authorities have found creative ways of ensuring representation, for example, by placing a bus in the middle of a town and asking children to leave a postcard with their views on it. Youth forums in schools are also involved in consultation over issues such as bullying and catering. Participation Works (Davey 2010) reports that over two thirds of the organisations they surveyed had a written policy or strategy to support participation, and consultation with groups of children took place most commonly in areas which had an obvious impact on their lives, such as leisure, recreation and play activities.

Factors to take into account in determining the means of participation

A number of different factors will affect the opportunities children and young people have to participate in decision-making forums and impact upon the choice of the most appropriate means. As already pointed out, the first are the ages and capacity of the children concerned. Second, attention needs to be paid to the context and arena in which the transactions are taking place. And third, decisions about the most appropriate means also depend upon what resources are available at the time.

Different levels and means of participation are effective for different groups of children and young people. Groups who are socially excluded, such as children with disabilities and children from minority ethnic groups, will experience particular difficulties in participating.

Age

Article 12 of the UNCRC stresses that due weight be given to the age and maturity of the child. While a standardised view of the stages of 'normal' children's development and linked capacity can provide a useful starting point for considering when a child is 'old enough' to participate and how, in considering the most appropriate means of involvement maturity cannot be determined by applying standardised norms.

Starting with age, as we all know, children differ hugely in their experience, intelligence and capacity to understand what is going on, especially in relation to the structures set up by adults, for adults. Some children at puberty are less able to know or to communicate their wishes than some 5-year-olds. Indeed, on top of the child's abilities, much depends upon the enabler. Their skills and their relationship with the child will profoundly influence what the child can know and say.

There are difficulties in ensuring that the views of younger children are sought at all. Evans and Fuller (2006) discuss these in relation to pre-school children. They point out that the power differential is particularly potent here, as are ethical issues around informed consent. And, returning to the situation of children in court, approximately 60 per cent of children who are the subject of care proceedings are under the age of 6. While a recent judgement in the Court of Appeal in *Re M* (2007) held that it was undesirable that a child should have to give evidence in care proceedings, and particular justification would be required before that course is taken, proponents, including at government levels, believe children should have a greater say in family courts and should be told by the judge what has been decided. The conclusion of the above Appeal was that it may be that the child's future cannot be satisfactorily determined without the child giving evidence. This leaves open the means of executing this.

Fortunately there is now greater recognition that young children should be offered opportunities to participate. In 2006 the Education Minister tabled an amendment to the Children Act (2004) requiring local councils to have regard to views of children under 5 years.

Turning to involvement in organisational activities, the age of the children should not necessarily preclude them from taking part. While it may be unrealistic to expect young children to manage a project to the end, they can initiate it and their views be instrumental in its management, delivery and the final outcome. Rafferty (2006) describes a project in Scotland where primary school children advised about a range of issues in the playground, effecting substantial change in the way playground time was then organised. However, these children did not manage the project to the end, if at all.

Disability

As with age, there are a number of difficulties in ensuring the views of children with disabilities are sought and included both in individual decision making, and in organisational planning. A survey of social services departments in England (Sinclair and Franklin 2000) revealed that the participation of disabled children was not sustained across all departments and lagged behind that of non-disabled children. At a high strategic level it was rare. Franklin and Sloper (2009) raises a further point: that disabled children may lack the opportunity even to participate in everyday activities, such as social activities, let alone be able to actively participate in decision making.

An additional disadvantage faced by children with disabilities is that they are a marginalised group. They are significantly more vulnerable to abuse than non-disabled children, and eight times more likely to be in care (NSPCC 2003). And they may have particular difficulties in mobility and communication. Thus their capacity to participate is reduced while at the same time they are largely dependent upon the knowledge, skills and sensitivity of adults to choose the best means of effecting their participation.

In addition to the communication techniques used with children with disabilities described earlier in this chapter, Franklin and Sloper (2009) portrays a technique she used with deaf children. In her deaf services project children were asked to draw a 'map' or diagram of all the people who help them when they are upset. Their questions for the service providers were written down on brightly coloured pieces of paper, and then the children were helped to write down their answers.

The Mosaic approach (Clark and Moss 2001), using observation, cameras, tours and mapping, provides multi-modal means of communicating with children who may have reduced language and communication. And there are now, also, a number of computer programmes specifically designed for children with disabilities. In My Shoes (Calam *et al.* 2005) is a computer package designed to help children with learning disabilities to communicate about potentially distressing experiences. The programme includes sound, speech and video material to help to provide a structure for the interviews.

It should be reiterated here, however, that this dependency on adults is itself problematic. A Department of Health report (2003, p.72) concluded that, although councils had consulted service users, it was mainly the parents of disabled children who responded. Where children with disabilities is concerned the difficulties of getting the views of the child without the parent's input impact upon research as well as in practice (see Mitchell *et al.* 2009).

Ethnicity

Communication barriers also affect the capacity of children whose first language is not English to participate. Their engagement and representation might be dependent upon a relative or friend, or on translators or on interpreters. Chand's (2005) description of the role of interpreters in child protection social work with minority ethnic families in the UK well illustrates the difficulties of the interpreting process:

> It is not enough to simply have an interpreter who can speak the appropriate language: the concepts associated with child maltreatment and neglect are very different from those concerning welfare benefits... interpreters who are competent in the latter might find themselves at a loss when trying to interpret terms around child abuse. (p.819)

Even where the children themselves speak English, language and culture can create barriers to their engagement. Chong (2006) illustrates this point in her account of the situation of a 14-year-old Chinese boy, Tony. Tony lived with his parents, grandmother and two brothers in a takeaway shop in an inner-city area. The school referred him to children's services following his disclosure that his father forced him to work in the shop and had threatened him with a knife. Only Tony's father spoke English, and he resented the social worker's attempts to talk to the family. Tony's mother and grandmother did not speak English, and they also avoided the social worker who they saw as a 'figure of authority'. Tony was thus in a family environment which did not recognise nor wish him to speak about his suffering. When the social worker visited the home he denied anything was amiss, and his family refused to co-operate. His social worker was unable to involve him in any direct work or decision-making process.

Children's maltreatment

Sticking with groups who are socially excluded, the last group to consider here is children who have been subject to abuse. Their maltreatment can embrace physical, emotional and sexual abuse and neglect, and ranges from harm caused by parents or carers to exploitation and collective harm inflicted by gang warfare, disaster and so on. Article 19 of the UNCRC thus includes: 'all forms of physical or mental violence, injury and abuse, neglect or negligent treatment, maltreatment or exploitation, including sexual abuse'.

In England in 2009, 547,000 children were referred to social services for abuse, of whom 34,100 became the subject of a child protection plan. Of those, by far the largest number, 15,800, were registered as suffering from neglect, 9100 from emotional abuse, 4400 from physical abuse, 2000 from sexual abuse and 2900 from mixed abuse. Although the numbers subject to a child protection plan have increased by nearly 10,000 over the last five years, this measurement is an under-estimate since much is unreported or remains unsubstantiated due to lack of evidence.

Children who have been abused have suffered a violation of their right to protection, and this will make it more difficult for them to exercise their right to participate in the decision-making arenas in child protection work. Many have lost trust in adults. Many are emotionally disturbed and frightened. Some want nothing to do with social workers at all. These children face particular difficulties in their attempts to be heard, such as stressful meetings and court appearances, fear of reprisal and several changes of social worker. More detail of their experiences of representation is contained in Chapter 7, which reports on children's participation in child protection investigations.

Finally, I will now look in more detail at two further factors that need to be taken into account in considering methods of effecting children's participation. First are a range of issues about how the adults involved determine and interpret what the child is saying and meaning. Second, the context, location and time in which participatory activities take place need to be taken into account in considering children's capacity and desire to speak up and engage.

Determining meaning and interpreting

While it is clearly important to include the views of all children, issues arise over how the child's meaning is interpreted and the ways in which more indirect communications can affect the transaction between messenger and receiver – as well as the message received. The literature on research with children (Christensen and James 2000; Hallet and Prout 2003) has highlighted the complexity of interpreting the meaning of what children say. Children, like adults, use language differently. Sinclair *et al.* (2002) report on a government study where children interpreted the word 'protection' to mean over-protection in the form of restrictions set by adults. This was seen negatively, whereas, in contrast, 'being safe' was viewed positively.

Similar difficulties apply to the use of interpreters where children do not speak English (see Chand 2005). Meanings of words – especially technical ones – can be confused or wrongly interpreted. Additionally, children who have been abused may have been too frightened to tell the truth to the adults advocating for or representing them. And, as the earlier discussion on advocacy suggested, even in individual decision-making arenas, such as family group conferences, it cannot always be taken for granted that advocates accurately represent what the child wants.

Social workers have a duty to ensure the views of the child are heard. However, many children, irrespective of their age, struggle to articulate or put into words what has happened to them and it is often only through play, drama or drawings that children can begin to express their views. For children who have communication difficulties or learning disabilities, or who do not speak English, the problems are compounded. Questions of interpretation arise when the only evidence of what a child wants to communicate is through symbols, creative writing, drawings and so on. Is it acceptable for professionals to interpret the meaning of the child's representation – for example, of a drawing? How do we know the adult's interpretation is correct, and should it be acted upon? In decision-making arenas, such as child protection conferences or courts, decisions have to be made which take into account the best possible evidence of the child's views. But in some cases this is based on the adult's interpretation, and the child's view is what the adult says it is.

Context, location and time

As discussed in relation to the different arenas in which participation in the UK takes place, context also has to be taken into account in determining the most effective means of participation. Whatever the setting, the timing and location of the activity is important. Children need to feel comfortable and they need to feel safe. Frightening environments – be they in the home, for example where domestic violence has taken place, or in alien settings such as courts – will make children reluctant to engage.

Returning to considerations of children in court, the ways in which children are involved in family proceedings continue to be a contentious issue. Judges are currently being asked to see children in family proceedings, but there are continuing concerns about the impact on children of being asked their views of their parents' behaviour in court by a judge. Some judges think they should be present in court if they wish to be; others that the judge should see them privately; others that that is the role of the Children's Guardian. This raises issues about advocacy and the use of intermediaries, as discussed earlier: should children be present in such an alien environment, or represented through an intermediary, such as a Guardian, or both?

Recent research by the NSPCC, *Your Shout Too!* (2007), suggests children do want more involvement in the court process, but also recognises that not all children want to participate directly. As a result a number of 'trailblazer' courts are being set up which seek to establish good practice in listening to children including by the judge. Their representation by Children's Guardians is also to be monitored.

Turning to the effect of time on children's opportunities to participate, traditionally, social work was carried out in office hours. The practitioners would determine when work will take place, meaning children's opportunity to choose a time that suits them is limited. An advantage of internet communication means that children may be able to choose times that suit them, as well as setting up situations which may be more private, anonymous and less intimidating than, say, an office. Ferguson's (2009) description of the work done by social workers with children during car journeys also evidences how more informal settings can enable children to speak more freely. Working with children in informal settings, such as at a cafe, or on walks with the dog, can also enable children to speak with more confidence so that the social worker or advocate can hear their views and discuss how best to present them to a wider audience.

In this chapter we have looked at the advantages and disadvantages of differing means of representing children, from their physical presence to representation, advocacy and consultation. The next chapter outlines the background to the rights agenda, and describes how the policy has developed in the UK.

CHAPTER 3

The Policy and Background to Children's Participation

We turn now to look in more detail at what the rights agenda comprises, what has promoted its acceptance in the UK, and what policies there are in place to support it. Acceptance of children's participation has been fuelled by the convergence of new and developing ideas coming from several different perspectives. In addition to the new paradigms within social science that have increased our understanding of the child as a competent social actor, two others have been of particular importance: the influence of the consumer movement and the children's rights agenda.

The consumer movement

The consumer movement first came to prominence in the 1970s and is now reflected in terms like 'user involvement'. The role of 'user' now includes children and young people. The involvement of users has succeeded in so far as consumers have more power in exercising their preferences and in influencing the nature and quality of the goods and services made available to them. Indeed the consumer or user mandate for participation now stretches beyond the concerns of individuals to the impact on users collectively (Braye 2000). It also challenges policy making and resource allocation for service provision.

The influence of users in respect of public services was initially emphasised by the UK government's Modernising Agenda (Department of Environment, Transport and the Regions 1998; Department of Health 1998) and, as will be described in this chapter, has been substantially developed over the last decade.

The rights agenda

Children are now specifically included within the rights agenda. The UNCRC (United Nations 1989, p.1) lays out three related rights:

- to the provision of services
- to protection and care, and
- to participate in society and decision making at both political and individual level.

In 1991 the UK government adopted the UNCRC. The Convention declares that children have human rights as individuals in their own right. It gives them rights to participate in decisions that affect them, most notably through Article 12 (see later in this chapter). However the UNCRC also recognises that children may be vulnerable by placing children's rights to participate alongside their need for protection and the provision of services (Lansdown 1995). In doing so it went a considerable way to deflect the former paternalistic notions that accepting responsibility for someone resulted in taking responsibility away from him. As has been said:

> Participation is the keystone of the arch that is the UNCRC. Without the active participation of children and young people in the promotion of their rights to a good childhood, none will be achieved effectively. (Badham quoted in Willow 2002, p.6)

Alongside these developments, a number of events in the UK have shaped the legislative framework for children in the social care sphere.

Public inquiries and serious case reviews

A series of inquiries into children's deaths in England brought home to the public in general, and health and welfare agencies in particular, that *not only were children not being listened to, but also that their protection depended upon hearing their stories.*

As early as 1974, the death of Maria Colwell laid bare the problems that arise from not listening to the child. Maria was killed by her stepfather despite having spoken loudly about her fears of him and her wish to be with her own family. The 1975 Children Act included, for the first time, the requirement to ascertain the wishes and feelings of children when making decisions about them.

The similarities with the death of Victoria Climbié 30 years later, and more recently the deaths of Peter Connelly (2007) and Khyra Ishaq (2009) reinforce the message that hearing children's voices is integral to their protection, and that the view that adults both know best and will act in their best interests has failed many children (Lansdown 1995). Serious case reviews (Brandon *et al.* 2008) have tracked the reasons for child deaths, and in each case demand a sharper focus on the child and the child's views. Where children are not being seen alone – especially where this is a recurrent aspect of a pattern – there is danger.

> A recurrent issue is the virtually complete failure to seek, far less establish, the wishes and feelings of each child of the household… [the mother] effectively prevented any direct individual contact with the children, even when this was belatedly attempted by the social worker. The protection plan did not include any contingency arrangements to address this failure in assessment. (p.91)

The Gillick case

The Gillick case was one of two key events which brought home *the need to begin to find ways of balancing parents' and children's rights.*

This case in 1986 formed a watershed in the changing balance of power between adults and children, and was an open acknowledgement that parental rights are not universal. The Gillick case was brought by a parent disputing the doctor's right to prescribe contraception for young people under 16 without parental consent. In focusing on the issue of consent rather than on 'parental rights' or parental powers, the court held that in some circumstances a minor could consent to treatment, and that a parent had no power to veto treatment. Lord Scarman required that a child could consent if they fully understood the medical treatment being proposed. Further, a child who is deemed 'Gillick competent' can prevent their parents viewing their medical records.

> Parental rights yield to the child's right to make his own decisions when he reaches a sufficient understanding and intelligence to be capable of making up his own mind on the matter requiring a decision. (Per Lord Scarman in *Gillick v West Norfolk and Wisbech Area Health Authority and Another* 1986, AC.112, at 186)

The Cleveland Inquiry

The second of these key events occurred in the following year. The Cleveland Inquiry, which took place in 1987 (see Cleveland Report 1988), reinforced concerns about the balance between parents' and children's rights. The draconian removal of 121 children from their parents highlighted that acting upon absolute concepts of rights may not necessarily be in the child's best interests. Attention was focused on the balance between family and state, and on whether the child's best interests would, in fact, be better met by the state than by their parents. Following parents' objections a number of the children were returned home. As a result, the subsequent Children Act 1989, discussed below, endeavoured to ensure that both children and their parents had a right to be heard in major decision-making forums. A central principle of the Act was to move to a social work approach of negotiating with families and children – working in partnership with them.

The UNCRC

These years also witnessed powerful *international influences to strengthen the rights of children.*

The ratification of the UNCRC by the UK government in 1991 was the first piece of international legislation to acknowledge that 'children are subjects of rights rather than merely recipients of protection'. As Kirby *et al.* (2003) point out, this acceptance encouraged services to recognise that this required working with children and young people rather than for them and understanding that acquiring responsibility for someone does not mean taking responsibility away from them.

The UNCRC places a duty on government and professionals to obtain and act upon the views of young people regarding the services they receive. Article 12 of the Convention states that:

> State parties shall assure to the child who is capable of forming his or her own views the right to express those views freely in all matters affecting the child, the views of the child being given due weight in accordance with the age and maturity of the child… For this purpose, the child shall in particular be provided the opportunity to be heard in any judicial and administrative proceedings affecting the child, either directly, or through a representative or an appropriate body, in a manner consistent with the procedural rules of national law.

In addition to enforcing children's rights to express their views on matters that affect them, Article 13 acknowledges that children's preferred ways of communicating may differ from adults and should be respected.

> The child shall have the right to freedom of expression: this right shall include the freedom to seek, receive and impart information and ideas of all kinds, regardless of frontiers, either orally, in writing or in print, in the form of art, or through any media of the child's choice.

Article 3.3 states that in all actions concerning children, their best interests shall be the primary consideration and Article 36 enforces their right to protection from all forms of exploitation.

The social exclusion agenda

A more recent development is that: *concerns about children and young people's disillusionment* with political engagement have contributed to the government's desire to include them in decision-making processes at a community as well as an individual level.

The Crick Report, by the Advisory Group on Citizenship (1998), was an initial response in the UK to concerns about young people's disengagement from their wider society. Such disengagement continues to be seen as being evidenced by the fact that they do not vote, by their educational failure, teenage pregnancy, substance abuse, racist behaviour, vandalism…and so on.

A growing body of literature refers to the 'culture of disaffection' that exists among children and young people due to the government's failure to respond to their specific needs (see Jack and Gil 2010). And as children's participation is now seen as being central to the social exclusion agenda, keeping them on board is regarded as being key to reducing delinquent anti-social behaviour and to producing 'good' adults.

Education for citizenship has been seen as one means of promoting children and young people's involvement in responsible community-minded activities – as being essential to achieving social inclusion. However, whether education for citizenship in schools is being effective remains to be seen. The Education and Skills Select Committee evaluated the situation in 2007, and reported that the quality and extent of citizenship education was inconsistent across England and

Wales, and that the approach was 'light touch'. They believed that the citizenship curriculum should focus on issues of identity, diversity and belonging, and that school councils should encourage involvement and ownership across the community.

School councils are seen as having a central part to play in citizenship education. In support of making their role statutory, the Connexions service, which initially had a Young Charter for local schools to develop the involvement of young people in decision making, more recently focuses on advising 13–19-year-olds on future careers and employment. And awards such as the UNICEF Respecting Schools Award support schools in teaching about 'children's and human rights and modelling rights and respect in all relationships between pupils and between pupils and teachers and adults' (DCSF 2008a, p.6).

The legislation

The last three decades have thus witnessed increasing recognition and acceptance of the rights of children and young people to participate in decisions that affect them, as well as an acknowledgement by organisations that children and young people's views need to be included in the planning and delivery of services. The ensuing legislation and guidance in the UK has reflected and developed this process.

The Children Act (1989)

The Children Act (1989) was a key piece of legislation informing practice in social service departments. It still provides the overall framework for consulting and involving children in a range of arenas, and places on local authorities the following duties:

- to ascertain the wishes and feelings of children and young people (having regard to their age and understanding) and take these into account before any Care Plans or court decisions are made

- to invite them to attend or participate actively in reviews and other planning meetings

- to notify them of decisions that have been reached at planning and review meetings

- to inform them of what services and resources are available to them.

(Department of Health 1991, p.64)

The principles of the Act thus include consulting with children and young people, taking their views into account, involving them in meetings and reviews and keeping them informed. Key sections are Sections 22(4)a and 22(5)a, which require local authorities to consider the wishes and feelings of any child who is, or may be, looked after, and to establish complaints procedures. And Section 1(3) requires courts to do the same in respect of all children involved in legal proceedings. Working Together (Department of Health 1991) provided concrete proposals as to how this should be effected in a range of forums, including informing them of their rights and of the options available to them. The Act thus strengthened the child's right to be involved in decisions and statutory processes at all stages from assessment through to review, both in court proceedings and more informally. For example when aged 16, a young person can consent to the provision of accommodation for herself, irrespective of the parents' wishes (Children Act 1989, Section 20(11)).

However, while this Act placed specific obligations on local authorities and courts to ascertain children's wishes and feelings when taking decisions regarding their welfare, Lyon and Parton (1995) suggest that this section of the Act lacks clarity with regard to the weight to be attached to children's versus adults' views. For example, in complaints and review procedures for looked-after children, adults with parental responsibility have the same entitlements. The child's view is thus not the only influencing factor, and the weight of the child's view is left open to interpretation. Likewise, in court proceedings it is the court and not the child who has the final say. And, in relation to the child's right to refuse a medical or psychiatric assessment, that refusal can be over-ridden where there is evidence that they lack 'sufficient understanding' of the request.

In 1996 the Family Law Act extended the requirement to consider children's wishes and feelings to private as well as public law.

The Human Rights Act (1998) and Quality Protects (1998)

The requirements that young people should be involved in decision-making processes were further strengthened by the Human Rights Act (1998). This encouraged a human rights culture in social care organisations and placed young people's participation centrally within the Quality Protects programme (a government initiative to transform services for children in need; see Department of Health 2001). A key component of Quality Protects (QP), supported by the QP Children and Young People's Participation Project Team, was to achieve active participation as well as active listening. Quality Protects (Objective 8) required local authorities to set performance indicators in relation to involving users and carers in planning services and tailoring packages of care and to ensure effective mechanisms are in place to handle complaints (including developing advocacy services). The objectives are specifically to demonstrate that the views of children and families are actively sought and used in planning, delivery and review of services, and to demonstrate that the satisfaction of users with the services provided is increasing.

The Framework for the Assessment of Young People and their Families (2000)

The Framework for the Assessment of Young People and their Families and accompanying guidance (Department of Health 2000) further set out ways in which policy could be informed, including by establishing children's forums and appointing a Children's Champion. Five key tasks for working with children were identified: seeing, observing, engaging, talking and activities. The 1999 document was revised in 2006 following the Children Act (2004), and this specifically required the involvement of children and young people in assessments, child protection conferences and reviews, family group conferences and looked-after children's reviews. A child-centred approach is defined in the following way:

> The child is seen and kept in focus throughout the assessment and… account is always taken of the child's perspective. (Department of Health 1999, Section 1.34)

Every Child Matters (2003)

Every Child Matters (DfES 2004a) reported following Lord Laming's Report (2003) on the Climbié inquiry. It sets out a new approach to the wellbeing of children, the overall aim being for every child to have the support they need to be healthy, stay safe, enjoy and achieve, make a positive contribution and achieve economic wellbeing. All organisations providing services for children should work together, and children and young people should have more say in issues that affect them both as individuals and collectively. To achieve this every local authority is to create a Children's Trust to encourage all partners to work together, and to involve children and young people in the process. The Children Act (2004) sets out the legislative frameworks for these objectives to be achieved.

The Children Act (2004)

This Act provides the legislative framework for the *Every Child Matters* recommendations. It amends Sections 17, 20 and 47 of the Children Act (1989) to ensure that, as far as is possible, children's wishes and feelings are taken into consideration where actions affect them and in relation to the services to be provided. The appointment of a Children's Commissioner for England under the Children Act (2004), Sections 10–14, is intended to further promote this process by raising awareness of the need for government to respond to children's voices. His role is to ensure that all the agencies working with children understand and are aware of their views, and to encourage people working with children to take into account their views and interests.

One way in which this has recently been affected is by the setting up in 2010 of an organisation by the Children's Commissioner, 11 Million, designed as a medium through which children and young people can make their voices heard, especially through web-based initiatives.

The desire for agencies to seek children's views on their services was further developed by the requirement in the Act that Children's Trusts set up mechanisms for seeking children's views and participation. Children's Trusts were designed by government to provide a framework for all agencies working with children to work together; 'to make England the best place in the world for children and young people to grow up in' (DCSF 2007b, p.4). They have three core features; long-term objectives covering the *Every Child Matters* outcomes; a children's services Director in overall charge for delivering the outcomes and a single planning and commissioning function sorted by pooled budgets (see Brayne and Carr 2008).

The Children and Young People's Plan (2007)

The Children's Plan: Building Brighter Futures (DCSF 2007b) specifically requires every Children's Trust to create a three-year Children and

Young People's Plan, setting out their vision for their services and how the views of the children and young people in the locality will feed in to it. As an example, in 2009 one Children's Trust drew up a consultation document in a number of different formats, including a toolkit which was distributed by their Play Team during the holiday activity programme to enable practitioners to lead consultation exercises. Four thousand children and young people took part through events such as conferences for school councils, focus groups about specific issues and specially commissioned pieces of research. In addition a young person's panel was recruited to support the consultation. Some of the key points raised by the young people included their concerns about the effect of pollution from cars, their desire for more information about healthy eating and sexual health and their wish for more school counselling. Concerns about bullying in schools also featured, reflecting the concerns raised by young people in another location and described in Chapter 9.

Working Together to Safeguard Children (2010)

Following the death of Peter Connelly in 2007, the 2006 Working Together guidance (HM Government 2006) was updated to address a further 23 of Lord Laming's recommendations (2009). Lord Laming reiterated the importance of professionals 'getting to know children as individual people' (Section 1.15). To keep the child in focus he made the following recommendations, which were subsequently written into Working Together 2010:

- developing a direct relationship with the child

- obtaining information from the child about his or her situation or needs

- eliciting the child's wishes and feelings – about their situation now as well as their plans and hopes for the future

- providing children with honest and accurate information about the current situation, as seen by professionals, and future possible actions and interventions

- involving children in key decision making

- providing appropriate information to the child about his or her rights to protection and assistance

- inviting children to make recommendations about the services and assistance they need and are available to them

- ensuring children have access to independent advice and support (for example through advocates or children's rights officers) to be able to express their views and influence decision making

- the importance of eliciting and responding to the views and experiences of children is a defining feature of staff recruitment, professional supervision, performance management and the organisation's broader aims and development.

(DCSF 2010, p.33)

In response, the final report of the Social Work Task Force, *Building a Safe and Confident Future* (2009), recommended a more coherent and effective national framework for continuing professional development, with a focus on improving social work practice with children and families, and the structures they have recommended, such as a probationary year following training, are currently being put into place (Recommendation 9).

Other policy

Other government Codes and associated legislation inform participatory practice. The early work of the Children and Young People's Unit (CYPU), established in 2000, produced *Learning to Listen: Core Principles for the Involvement of Children and Young People* (2001), which furthered the commitment to listening to the views of children and young people in the social care sector:

> The government wants children and young people to have more opportunities to get involved in the design, provision and evaluation of policies and services that affect them or which they use. (Children and Young People's Unit 2001, p.4)

The Adoption and Children Act (2002) placed a duty on local authorities to provide advocacy services to children who wish to complain. Following this many local authorities developed their complaints service, with complaints officers playing a pivotal role in engaging with complainants and their advocates (see Parry *et al.* 2008).

Looked-after children and young people

In relation to looked-after children there has been a gamut of specific guidance and recommendations. For example, the *UK National Standards for Foster Care*, which were produced by The Fostering Network (1999), were underpinned by a commitment to developing foster care services, including by consultation with young people. The Care Standards Act (2000) included regulations requiring that information about services be made available to children and young people in a variety of accessible formats. The LAC circular 22 (LAC 2000) required local councils to involve young people collectively and to enhance their individual voices through, for example, the development of advocacy services.

In 2002 the National Minimum Standards for Children in Care were introduced (Department of Health 2002b). They require that 'the views of children...are taken into account in the development of necessary changes in the operation of the home' (Section 8.11, p.22). This was followed by *Care Matters: Time to Deliver for Children in Care* (DCSF 2008b). Under the Care Matters agenda, the voice of the child is identified as the foundation of excellent corporate parenting, alongside high aspirations and stable relationships. All councils should consult with children effectively.

More recently, the Children and Young Persons Act (2008) laid down clear guidance for involving looked-after young people in the planning, design and delivery of children's services. Currently these standards are under review but the National Children in Care Councils Initiative that began in 2009 continues to support local authorities in providing a forum for young people to express their views, share their experiences and influence the services that affect them. As a result councils now make a Council Pledge to children in care. In their pledge, Bristol City Council, for example, pledges to 'make sure you have an independent reviewing officer to help plan with you...and check that the plans are carried out every six months' (Bristol City Council 2009, p.5).

The Children's Fund, Sure Start and Connexions

Turning to the preventative agenda, in England the Children Act (2004), the Children's Fund, Sure Start and Connexions initiatives all required services to demonstrate how they had included the views of children and young people in their development and delivery. Sure

Start programmes included parents on their committees and they fed in the views of the children using the facilities. Like Sure Start, the Children's Fund initiative had participation as a guiding principle, and this also involved children and parents in producing a map of local needs and services and in determining the gaps in existing provision.

Health

Following the publication in 2003 of *Every Child Matters* (DfES 2003b), the National Service Framework for Children (Department of Health 2003) was set up. Both claimed that their overall goals were based on consultations with children. The National Service Framework for Children, Young People and Maternity Services (Department of Health 2004) stresses the need to take children's views into account and sets out guidance on how this should be achieved:

> At the heart of this National Service Framework is a fundamental change in our way of thinking about children's health. It advocates a shift with services being designed and delivered around the needs of the child. Services are child-centred and look at the whole child... (Department of Health 2004, p.2)

One example is by ensuring information is adequate and accessible, and by offering treatment choices, including for those with complex health needs. Other aims include professionals communicating directly with children and a service which is child-centred and responsive to the child's individual and developing needs. Furthermore the views of children need to be taken into account and valued at all stages of service delivery (Department of Health 2003). Specifically, feedback on the care and services children and young people receive is highlighted. Most recently, in acknowledging the particular difficulties faced by children with disabilities, the Disabled Children Review, which was part of the Comprehensive Spending Review (2007), referred to the importance of gaining the perspectives of disabled children.

Education

In schools, the Education Act (2002) provided guidance on young people's participation in school activities. This was developed in 2004 by *Working Together: Giving Children and Young People a Say* (DfES 2004c) and in 2007 by *Aiming High for Young People: A Ten-year Strategy for Positive Activities* (DCSF 2007). This White Paper included a section on 'empowerment', including the extension of the Youth Opportunity and Capital Funds, the intention of giving young people influence over 25 per cent of spending on youth activities by 2018, and an expectation that local authorities will adopt good practice in engaging young people.

The publication in 2010 of *Working Together to Safeguard Children* laid out in detail some of the ways in which young people should be participating in school governance and management, for example, by setting up youth councils which would send electives to the UK Youth Parliament, by involvement in staff appointments and by lesson observation. Their role in supporting peers was also supported through mechanisms for peer support, peer mentoring and peer mediation.

Having outlined the policies in place for supporting children's participation in public arenas, such as schools and councils, as well as in individual decision making, we turn next to look at the theories and conceptual frameworks that underpin participatory policy and practice.

CHAPTER 4

The Theoretical Principles that Underpin Participatory Practice

To work with children and young people effectively – to help them to speak and to take part in the complex social work interventions described later in this book, such as initial child protection conferences where a range of professionals discuss in detail the child's abuse or neglect by their carers and their future care – social workers draw upon a range of concepts and theories. Knowing and using theories of child development is crucial in enabling practitioners to understand children, make sense of their lives and work with them in age-appropriate ways. Other theories most commonly used and underpinning participatory and empowering practice are attachment theory, systems and ecological theories, and sociological theories of childhood. This chapter describes these theories, looks at how they are used in practice and suggests some of their shortcomings.

Traditionally, social work has been informed by psychological theories based on biological phases and conceptions of the importance of family dynamics, in particular parent–child attachment relationships, in determining children's behaviour in the here and now as well as in adulthood. As outlined earlier, there is strong evidence from many studies of children's experiences of involvement in social work decisions made about their lives that the concept of attachment to a trusted person is key to their capacity to engage and participate.

More recently sociological theories have stressed the need to see children as individuals with rights of their own, as having agency and as being competent to make their own choices. Within this framework children's views can and should be seen as standing alongside those of their adult carers and informing decision making effectively.

And ecological theories add what has been a missing link to the picture by highlighting the impact community and environment have upon the opportunities and facilities available to the children and young people themselves as well as to the practitioners who work with them. In enabling children and young people to participate social workers draw upon all of these theories. Each has shortcomings; taken together they are complementary.

Psychological theories

Psychological and psychoanalytic theories of child development have had, and continue to have, a major influence on social work with children and families. Freud's (1923) theory of child and personality development was based on biology – on innate and invariant drives which he described in terms of five psychosexual stages from birth (oral stage) through to the onset of puberty (genital stage). While it is also important to take into account that children's development is determined by a range of factors and not static at any one point in time, there is agreement that the biological stages in child development, such as dependency needs in early childhood, are universal. Familiarity with developmental norms thus underpins all judgements about the most appropriate means of communication. Effective communication between social worker and child is, of course, the starting point for any engagement that underpins participatory practice.

In considering the most appropriate ways of gaining children's views and of determining the best means of their representation, the most effective ways of communicating with them thus have to be based on a solid knowledge and understanding of the child's age and maturity. For example, whereas conversation and discussion may be an appropriate way of gaining the views of adolescents, with young children games and play are likely to be more productive. The use of life-size puppets in the Webster Stratton parenting programme described in Chapter 1 provides a good example of an effective way of communicating with young children, but would be inappropriate with most adolescents where the use of computers may be more appropriate.

Erikson's life stage theory

Erikson (1968), most notably, expanded Freudian theory by adding a social dimension, and by locating critical stages of development across the whole life span. In working with children, Erikson's conceptualisation of life stages is extremely helpful in pointing up particular age-appropriate considerations and dilemmas. For example, in working with young people leaving care, who are struggling with issues of dependency, the concept of mastering the life stage split in adolescence between identity and role confusion can provide useful guidance for practitioners in enabling the young person to reach decisions about their future by focusing on self care skills, social networking and building self esteem. The findings from research studies of young people's experience of reviews, where key decisions are made about their future, highlight the need to ensure that young people's self esteem and confidence are sufficiently robust to enable them to feel included in these reviews which can determine their future.

A number of studies, including the one reported in Chapter 7, are common in reporting that young people do find it difficult to engage in reviews. Many say they feel bored and that the adults are making life decisions for them. A 14-year-old boy from this study said:

> 'I didn't think they were at all helpful – I was about 14 and they spoke to me as if I was a little kid – and that is what annoyed me.'

However, not all young people's experience of reviews is negative. Much depends upon how the review is chaired and the means by which the young person's participation is effected. An understanding, from Erikson's life stage theory, of the young person's emotional needs at this stage in their lives, and of how their previous experiences affect them, can give practitioners and the chairperson the knowledge upon which to base their practice in such decision-making arenas.

Piaget's cognitive theory

Piaget's (1959) cognitive theory also relates to biological development. He, like Erikson, describes development in a series of sequential stages in which the child's capacity for developing thought and integrating experience goes through stages of assimilation and accommodation. The first is from birth to 18 months (sensorimotor intelligence); the second to age seven (pre-operational); the third to adolescence (concrete operations); and the last from age 12 to 15 (final operations). Morality develops alongside the intellect in two stages representing the development of concepts of guilt and intention.

Piaget's theory can help, for example, in determining appropriate work with young children where it can be difficult for their views and wishes to be expressed and heard. In the pre-operational phase children cannot understand abstract concepts. The use of symbolic play or structured games are thus often the only means to access their wishes and feelings. In working with younger children who have experienced painful losses, such as loss of a parent through a care order or through divorce, games such as 'All About Me' (Hemmings, Smith and Pennells 1995) can help children approach these sensitive areas and express their feelings and wishes. In this colourful game, players make progress along a jungle path. The child and practitioner play the game together, taking turns to respond to statements printed on the set of cards, to help establish an atmosphere of trust. The practitioner is able to test out and clarify what the child is trying to say about who and what is important in her life, and so is enabled to represent the child's views in reviews, panel meetings and in court.

Bowlby's attachment theory

More recently, Bowlby (1969, 1988) built upon psychological theories by focusing in more detail on the impact of parent–child relationships on personality formation and social development. His attachment theory has proved to be robust and provides a valuable conceptual framework for analysing what children and young people find helpful in their relationships with social workers – trust and availability.

Attachment means an affectional bond, usually between a care giver and a care receiver. The four characteristics of attachment are:

- a safe haven
- a secure base
- proximity maintenance
- separation distress.

In early childhood the attachment requires that the child's dependency needs for safety, security and protection are met. Young children form attachments to a responsive and reliable care giver, generally the biological mother – but Bowlby later recognised that others could take on what he originally considered to be the 'mothering' role. He postulated that early experiences set up a system of thoughts and emotions about the self and others, called the 'internal working model', which continues to develop through adulthood. The internal working model regulates attachment-related behaviours and develops over time in response to the environment and to physical development, as well as to relationships with other key adults in the child's life, such as her social worker, teacher or carer. This is why the availability of a trusting and secure relationship with a professional can be important in the child's life and underpins good participatory practice.

Here a 16-year-old girl, as reported in Chapter 7, describes the importance of her relationship with her social worker:

> 'S was a nice person – a nice lass – with the right manner to go about it… She was concerned about me – it was like I could talk to her about problems if I had them…'

In middle childhood and adolescence, the need for proximity to the attachment figure shifts to emotional and physical availability as the child moves toward a greater degree of independence. The concept of emotional availability is particularly helpful to social workers working toward children's participation. We know, from studies of children's views, that what they value from their social worker is physical and emotional availability and that eliciting children's views can take time and skill.

The importance of a stable working relationship is strongly evidenced by the experiences of looked-after children. Many have several changes of worker in short spaces of time. Similar to the views of some of the young people in Chapter 9 who reflect on changes of worker, this 15-year-old girl portrays her sense of confusion and of feeling forgotten:

> 'She used to come every two weeks – then she stopped coming so much; after that she told us that she couldn't be our social worker any more because she had to go and work in a different place.'

Mary Ainsworth *et al.* (1978) expanded the theory's concepts following research on infant–parent pairs, and identified three attachment styles:

- secure
- anxious-avoidant (insecure)

- anxious-ambivalent or resistant (insecure).

Each of these patterns is associated with certain characteristic patterns of behaviour. Main and Solomon (1986) later added a fourth pattern: disorganised-disoriented attachment, reflecting the child's lack of a coherent coping strategy. Where children and young people's experience of care giving is unreliable or chaotic, children lack security, often developing defences which are avoidant and ambivalent. In these cases young people close down. Their sense of confusion may mean they struggle to understand and express their feelings and views, making it doubly difficult for social workers to hear and represent exactly what it is they want.

This quote about Rachel, a 17-year-old girl in Holland's (2010) study of looked-after children, well illustrates the difficulties in engagement that a series of practitioners are likely to experience – and how this prevents engagement:

> 'She's met her new one [social worker] once and thinks she seems OK, but said that's the third or fourth she's had since she's been in care. She said the other ones she's had were OK, but then went on to say that one was really young and inexperienced and so not much help to her. The first meeting they had the social worker didn't say anything, didn't instigate any conversations, so she just left making an excuse that she had to meet up with friends, 'cause she didn't want to take on the talking role herself.' (p.1675)

Attachment theory is thus particularly valuable in enabling us to understand why young people need to trust their social workers, carers and other key adults in their lives. It is only within the context of a secure and trusting relationship that children can assimilate information and make informed choices as to what their views are and how best to be represented. It is only by that route that young people can be enabled to exercise their rights to participation and service provision.

Sociological theories

Toward the end of the twentieth century a number of factors shifted the focus from psychological to sociological theories of understanding childhood. According to Smart, Neale and Wade (2001), sociologists 'rediscovered children'. Ariès' book, *Centuries of Childhood* (1962), became increasingly influential. He believed that, rather than viewing children as progressing simply through natural biological phases, childhood has to be located within the politics and culture prevailing – particularly in their early lives. This is not to deny the universality of developmental stages through the life course, but rather to insist that children's development is contingent upon the society and generation in which they live and thus the way they are regarded and treated by the adults who formulate the laws and policies that govern their lives. Children growing up in Ghana, for example, suffering from malnutrition, will have very different experiences and childhoods from those growing up in London or Glasgow. Nor is it to deny that children universally occupy a social space in their childhood, but rather to stress that its character is determined by context and culture, and is likely to change over time.

A sociological approach to childhood thus sees children as being social actors, as competent people with an informed and informing view of the world. Children are active agents who design their own lives, and who should therefore have a voice over decisions that are taken about them. And this concept of children as being unique supports that of Giddens (1991), who used the term 'individualisation'. This term allows us to see children as persons in their own right and with responsibilities, and is a driving force in social work practice in empowering children.

A concrete example of how this view of young people as active agents has influenced policy and practice is the establishment of the Young People's Councils and of the Youth Parliament in England in 2009. The Youth Parliament has 600 elected members, aged 11–18, who organise campaigns and projects and influence decisions on, for example, reducing the voting age to 16, cheaper bus fares for people under 18 and compulsory political education in schools.

Even where there is little evidence of effecting change, the experience of participating can enable children and young people to feel active and influential, as illustrated by Jack, a student who participated in the recent school protest against increased student tuition fees:

> 'It feels really brilliant to have some say in it all, to have some power over what is going on. We've had students who say this isn't going to get you anywhere. But where do they think saying this won't get you anywhere is going to get them?' (van der Zee 2010)

Sociological theories of childhood and children's rights have thus had a profound influence on the promotion of children's participation, particularly in national and international arenas where children's views are now actively sought, but also in encouraging practitioners working with children to treat them as adults, to take their views seriously and to work to promote their agency in decision-making arenas.

Ecology and systems theories

The ecological and systems theory constructed by Bronfenbenner (1979) also added an important environmental dimension to our understanding of child development which links to facilitating their capacity for involvement and participation in both community projects and individual decision-making processes. Jack and Gil (2010) stress the importance of connecting a range of environmental factors, such as housing, poverty, crime and schools in shaping children's lives alongside immediate family circumstances. They see the development of a culture of listening to children and adults and promoting partnership approaches to local provision as being central building blocks in community-oriented safeguarding practice because talking and listening to children sends out clear messages that their views are important to adults.

An example of how such an approach was successful in alerting professionals to safety issues is described by Nelson and Baldwin (2002). They set up a project in Craigmillar, called 'comprehensive neighbourhood mapping', in which children and young people identified risky places, people, situations and activities in their local communities which was fed back into local agencies and organisations to improve channels of communication and understanding between professionals as well as between the professionals and the children.

Ecology and systems theory thus adds an important social and community dimension to attachment theory which provides a conceptual understanding of the importance of relationship. It underlines the need to take into account the impacts that the children's environment and culture have on their capacity to engage and participate. And sociological theories of social constructions of childhood reinforce the need to treat all children as individuals with rights equal to adults, with agency and as having the capacity to be involved in decision-making forums.

These three theories provide a conceptual canvas for understanding children and they are complementary. They provide pointers to the most appropriate ways of communicating with children and working toward their participation. However, it is also important to take on board what shortcomings there may be in their application to participatory practice, especially in child protection work.

The shortcomings of the theories

While each of these theories provide, both separately and together, important understandings about what underpins and guides participatory practice, some difficulties and shortcomings remain. I start with a key and unresolved issue, faced particularly by professionals in child protection work, which neither psychological nor sociological theories can address satisfactorily – the issue of the ethics of care versus the ethics of rights. Central to this dilemma in relation to children's participation is the consideration of the imbalance of power between adults and children. I then move on to outline the shortcomings that appertain, first, to psychological theories and second, to sociological theories.

Needs versus rights/protection versus risk

In many practice situations there can be great difficulty in balancing children's wishes and rights against what the adults responsible for their care consider to be essential to the children's needs, including for safety. This is particularly pertinent to individual decision-making transactions, and in arenas where children's safety is at risk. It has been argued that concepts of need, upon which psychological theories are based, sit in opposition to concepts of rights, which are more within the domain of sociology, and so do not allow for a rights perspective to inform practice. There are real issues here in relation to age, ability and vulnerability, and between the consideration of children's rights and what adults might consider to be their needs, or, in other words, their best interests as determined by the adult. From one perspective an emphasis on needs could be seen to infantilise children because it derives from a desire to impose adult views. From another, an emphasis on rights could be perceived as neglectful or risky where possible harm would ensue.

Social workers in child protection cases stand in the middle of this dilemma: protection versus risk. In researching children's participation in child protection conferences, Shemmings (2000) poses the question: should the social workers stress the rights of children to be active participants, or rescue them from involvement in the face of possible harm? He interviewed 121 professionals in two authorities where children had been invited to attend the conference and found that, irrespective of whether they held a rights or a rescue perspective, their views were contradictory. Those who believed that children should not make decisions until they were much older also believed they should be invited to the conference.

The studies of children's involvement in child abuse inquiries and family group conferences that are presented in later chapters illustrate in more detail the conflict for practitioners between supporting children's rights to participate while ensuring their need for safety in decision-making arenas. Where a number of professionals are present, representing different agencies and carrying different roles, this can be particularly difficult to manage. Not all the professionals present know, or have even met the child; neither do they know necessarily what information has been shared with the child about her family.

To give an example, in one of the child protection conferences researched in Chapter 7, the solicitor unwittingly informed the conference, in the 11-year-old daughter's presence, that the mother had three adopted children from a previous relationship. This was news to the girl already traumatised by her abusive stepfather.

And again, quoting from an experience of a 14-year-old girl:

'I don't like it at all…being there…they talk about what's happened in the past and it brought it all back up.'

Power imbalance

Implicit in the above discussion is that there is no escape from issues of power. As Smart *et al.* (2001) and others have pointed out, participation, in itself, does not eradicate power differences. Efforts to encourage participation may promote a process of democratisation and power sharing between adults and children, but at the same time do not guarantee that both share the same view about the degree to which the views of the child should affect the decisions made. As is already abundantly clear, there are tangible and serious issues of power inherent in social work practice where safety is the practitioner's primary concern but may not be that of the child. Further, adult attitudes to children, as will be discussed later, profoundly affect all of our transactions with children, and will influence the dynamics of all of the participatory processes and outcomes described in this book.

Differences of opinion in relation to contact provide a good example of where the child's and the practitioner's views may be at variance. The child may desperately want to see her father, although the social worker knows that the father is likely to be difficult, violent and abusive toward her mother – and possibly also toward the child. The priority is the child's physical safety and emotional wellbeing, and it is the social worker's view – in this case that contact with the father is denied – that will carry. The social worker holds the power of decision making in many child protection arenas because of the need to prioritise safeguarding.

Conversely, a young person's involvement in the recruitment of a foster carer will include some components of power sharing. Her involvement would be based on having information about the applicants, it could be presented directly to the selection panel and the young person may be present in the interview and the subsequent discussion. These two situations exemplify different contexts, different levels of engagement and very different processes entailing very different opportunities for power sharing, all of which could affect the outcome.

Of course, as we know to our cost from previous public inquiries, it is essential to remember that the child can effectively hold the power in relation to sharing information that can influence a crucial decision. This is not uncommon in situations of domestic violence where either the child does not want to be removed from the home, or feels she is protecting her mother or carer by remaining silent. It is also a known aspect of sexual abuse, particularly where the child has been successfully groomed by her abuser and chooses not to disclose. Withholding information and distorting the facts can, in itself, be a means of exerting power.

A further aspect of power is identified by McLeod (2010). In interviewing young people in care, McLeod found that some felt alienated by their social worker's social class. The young people saw the power differential as being due to the social worker's social status, as well as to their real or imagined authority, and for them this was disempowering. The language the social worker uses, his dress, his style may all contribute to a sense of difference and alienation which militates against the young person's participation.

These examples well illustrate the tensions between children's rights to participate and the adult's responsibility to protect them from harm. The challenge for practitioners is to strike a balance between implementing a children's rights perspective, including the right to be heard and listened to in an appropriate and safe way, while continuing to offer appropriate care and protection, and this is acknowledged by the UNCRC. Whatever the balance, hearing what the children themselves say remains crucially important not only to protective but also to public health responses to their maltreatment.

I turn now to a critique of the psychological and sociological theories outlined above.

Critique of psychological theories
A deficit model

Psychological theories have been criticised for providing a deficit model of childhood, whereby children are seen as passive and dependent (Lee 2001) – as being in a state of becoming, rather than being. Clearly such a perspective could be patronising and make it more difficult to manage the already unequal balance of power between adult and child in decision-making arenas. This quote from a 13-year-old boy who was interviewed for the study about his experience of being present in a child protection conference well expresses his sense of disempowerment:

> 'I think they said they are doing check-ups on people like my friends – I felt like a prisoner in a way – not being able to do what I want in my own home.'

Furthermore, as suggested above, the focus on normative standards of development can detract from seeing children as individuals and addressing diversity. Professional assessments of children's development are now written on a number of electronic forms (the Integrated Children's System) developed from the Assessment Framework (Department of Health 2000). The assessments are based on normative standards which do not take into account a whole range of variables, such as ethnicity or disability. Children's needs and individuality can thus become lost at the point of assessment, and the narrative of their story hidden in standardised tick boxes.

This means both that practitioners fail to address the uniqueness of each child, and that the children are not encouraged to participate in the records that are kept about them (see Mitchell and Sloper 2009). Chapter 8 describes this process in more detail. Research (Shaw *et al.* 2009) of the use of the Integrated Children's System by practitioners evidences that service users, including children rarely see their records or contribute to them. The recording practice is not participatory, and it is of concern that such an approach could leak into other areas of practice. The end of the quote about Rachel (Holland 2010, p.1675) puts this succinctly:

> 'Her current support worker also seems more interested in form filling than in listening and chatting with her.'

Wellbeing and wellbecoming – a social investment?

Another criticism of psychological theories is that, from a developmental perspective, children are regarded as future citizens, to be educated, developed and shaped. Their wellbeing in the now will determine their wellbecoming in the future. Childhood is regarded as a preparation for adulthood and to ensure the stability of societal norms. In these terms children become a social investment and thus, it is argued, become valued by adults because of what they do, not who they are.

Again, the message for practitioners in enabling children's participation is to respond to their individuality and to enable them to declare their wishes in the here and now – even if they cannot be met or are out of line with what adults think may determine their future wellbeing or good behaviour. Butler *et al.*'s (2002) research on children's involvement in their parents' divorce clearly concludes with the importance of listening to what the children themselves say, not what their parents or society think best:

> Involving children in their parent's divorce…starts from a recognition that it is we (as adult professionals or simply as professional adults) who need to find our place in a complex personal and social dynamic in which children are already active participants rather than that they need to mesh in with systems, practices and procedures that

are designed to meet ends more allied to our particular interests and habits of thought. (p.100)

Another problem for children's participation raised by the social investment approach is discussed by Featherstone (2004). She points out that, although the social investment approach is targeted on children as a group, there is at the same time an identification of groups of children who pose a risk to the 'investment' project. Teenage mothers, looked-after children and boys from ethnic minority groups are seen to have characteristics which get in the way of their becoming responsible citizens. In the research study describing young people's contribution to decision-making processes in a local authority children's department (see Chapter 9), a number of groups of marginalised young people, such a travellers and Asian children, were significant by their absence. Such a feature was also found by the Participation Works survey in 2010. This can lead to a piecemeal approach to children's rights, where some groups of children and young people who are socially excluded find their views ignored because they are not regarded as valued future adults.

Cause and effect

Linked to this is another potential difficulty posed by the psychological model, that is, in determining the relationship between cause and effect – in this case, between what happens in childhood and successful adulthood. Psychological theories of childhood are supported by research on the relationship between problems in childhood and in later life (Bowlby 1977). As critics such as Jack and other ecologists cited above have argued, however, the relationship between cause and effect is by no means straightforward. Any number of factors occurring beyond parent–child early relationships, such as parental separation, acquired disability or peer group influences, can profoundly influence children's adaptations and behaviour. Clearly such factors need to be taken on board in any assessment of children's capacity, as the ecological approach suggests.

In considering a child's capacity to participate, the concept of resilience (Gilligan 2001) is helpful in enabling us to address the cause and effect issue. Resilience is located within 'normal' development, so whatever adversity children might have experienced, resilience is a protective factor which enables them to respond in positive ways, and to overcome or at least manage effectively experiences which might otherwise be damaging. Assessing children's resilience is thus an important factor for social workers in considering the most appropriate means of facilitating a child's participation in complex decision-making processes. The physical attendance of a young person at a review or meeting where sensitive issues are being discussed, for example, would be indicated if the young person is resilient. This is well illustrated by this 14-year-old girl's response when asked about her review in an interview for the study described in Chapter 7:

> 'I told them what I thought and I answered questions…they listened. I had some say in what was being decided… I asked him and my mum to have long weekends at home – and they arranged it.'

This experience of a review is in contrast with the more negative ones described above, illustrating the value for this girl of her physical presence at her review.

Critique of sociological theories
Autonomy versus responsibility
Turning to sociological theories, a critique of social constructions of childhood hinges on the view that children are autonomous, have agency and have rights. It could be argued that phenomena, such as autonomy and agency, depend entirely upon adults to be effected – and so are, themselves, limited by time, space, etc. This goes without saying in relation to statutory social work with children in need of protection, whereby the procedures by which they can be involved are determined by committees – Local Safeguarding Boards – not even by the practitioners themselves, and certainly not by the children and young people.

On a wider base – as Morrow (2001) points out – the worlds in which children live, especially beyond the arena of child protection, are not always determined by, dominated by or controlled by adults. To a degree children can organise their own lives in, for example, playgrounds. But here, again, exists the conflict between risk and safety, as we know from accounts of serious bullying taking place in outside spaces where adults are not in control.

Children as miniature adults

And finally, another problem raised by critics of the sociological approach is the risk that the responsibility and effort of involvement in complex decision making can mean children are denied their childhood and expected to respond as adults. Many of the procedures in child protection work, such as the recording systems described above and the structures and agendas of meetings, are constructed by adults, for adults. It could be damaging to assume that the children involved always have the capacity to understand and respond to some of the complex procedures and recording systems that are currently in place. The procedures and agenda for meetings, even for family group conferences where the agenda should in principle be left to the family to construct, provides a good example of the difficulty in the event of focusing on the child's agenda. For example, while some of the young people interviewed about their experiences of family group conferences, described in Chapter 6, said they had been asked who they would like to be at the meeting and what they thought should be discussed, others had not.

This chapter has described and reviewed the theories that contribute to practitioners' knowledge and skills in participatory practice. The concluding chapter in Part I moves on to look in more detail at the impact that environmental factors, adult attitudes to children and the culture of organisations have on children's opportunities to participate.

CHAPTER 5

What Gets in the Way?

Adult Attitudes, the World in which Children Live and Organisational Culture and Values

There are a number and range of barriers to empowering children to participate in decision making. At a global level, adult attitudes profoundly affect all of our attitudes to children, and so are influential in determining how far we want them to have a voice and be heard. Practitioners and managers are, of course, as much a part of the history and social structures that determine adult attitudes as anyone else. Indeed, there are many areas where society expects the professionals they employ to uphold their values and attitudes, despite professional judgement and commitment to anti-oppressive values. Public debates about adoption provide a good example of how social, religious and cultural attitudes and beliefs can inform policy and practice, and militate against children's wishes and views being sought with regards to which families they are placed with and ongoing family contact.

Turning to children's participation and the exercise of their rights to be involved, we have already touched on how the key issues of power imbalance and protection versus risk influence professional practice. In this chapter I would like to explore other influences on children's participation, and some of the impacts they have on policy and practice. Starting at the global level, I suggest some ways in which art, thought and literature have formed adult attitudes, and discuss the impact they have on the children themselves, on policy and on the ways in which research with children is conceived and conducted.

I then move on to describing how some aspects of the world in which children in the UK live today are disempowering, for the professionals as well as for the children. We might expect that children and young people living in developed countries which experience higher standards of living are better placed to assert their rights than those in developing countries. However, the reality is not straightforward. Adverse environments reduce the capacity of both the children and those that work with them to achieve empowering practice.

The last barrier to children's participation that impacts upon the practitioner's ability to engage in the time-consuming and skilled direct work necessary that I address here, is the culture and values of the organisations that employ them.

Adult attitudes
Depictions of childhood
Our attitudes to children are determined by a huge number of factors: our own childhood experiences of parenting, school and employment; our physical and mental capacities; our history and cultural background and the current world in which we live. We also carry with us powerful images from the past: from art, literature and philosophers. Butler and Williamson (1994) argue that the history of childhood is the history of adult myth-making about childhood – so childhood is what adults say it is. Art, literature and thought through the ages well demonstrate this by graphically illustrating how images of childhood change over time and in response to the political, cultural and economic conditions prevailing. It is also striking that the same tensions and issues surrounding power, innocence, dependency, care and control re-emerge and are ever present. The power of these on our actions and thinking as practitioners needs to be understood as it influences our work with children on both individual and organisational levels.

ART
Early portraits of children, such as 'Infant Marguerita in a Blue Dress' by Velasquez (1659), and 'Ter Borch Helena' by Van der Schalcke (1647) depict them as small adults – and that image continues from medieval times into the Renaissance period.

During the Age of Enlightenment, under the influence of Locke's 'Some Thoughts Concerning Education' (Locke 1960 [1693]), childhood was seen as a new beginning, as being reasonable and learned. Chodweick's illustration (1799) typified this image, with children looking reflectively into the sun in the distance – into the future. Portraits of children in the Romantic era, such as those by Phillip Otto Runge (1805) present them as reflecting the divine, with the features of angels.

Late Victorian portraits of children, such as those by Singer Sargent (1856–1925), present a more modern image of children as distinct individuals in the process of growing up. As the twentieth century progressed photography became the more common medium for pictures of children, reflecting both the development of technology and the shift to a much broader representational base and away from portraits of children commissioned by rich families.

LITERATURE

Literary portrayals of children have also profoundly influenced the way we visualise childhood. The Romantics, for example, celebrate the innocence of childhood in the face of corrupt adults. The Victorians also highlight children's frailty, and use this to expose adult and institutional corruption and brutality. Children, such as Oliver Twist, are portrayed as innocent, as having a separate nature from adults and inhabiting a separate world. The two main presentations of childhood in the nineteenth century thus reflect the cultural ambivalence of adversity and suffering on the one hand or a blissful, Edenic state on the other.

Literature in the twentieth century presents a more realistic and broad-based model of childhood in a world of change, while at the same time promulgating some of these earlier images. The increasingly complex world that children live in is communicated by many novels, including representations of childhood within diverse ideological and cultural contexts. Coetzee's *Boyhood* (1997) portrays the world of a boy aged from 7–13 in South Africa being invaded by the country's dramatic racial and political situation, with parents who try to be as English as possible in a community of Afrikaans. Many novels portray relationships between childhood and power – such as William Golding's *Lord of the Flies* (1954) and Margaret Atwood's narration of childhood trauma and survival, *Cat's Eye* (1989). *The God of Small Things* (Roy 1997) centres on what it feels like to be a child, to be small and powerless in front of what appear to be the overwhelming master narratives of history. The 7-year-old twins, Rahel and Estha, are 'trapped in the bog of a story that was and wasn't theirs' (p.224). Many texts are written from the child's point of view, with the child becoming an active participant in their stories and protagonists of their own lives. James Joyce's *A Portrait of the Artist as a Young Man* (1916) and Frank McCourt's *Angela's Ashes* (1996) are straightforwardly autobiographical, permeated by the question of identity.

PHILOSOPHERS

Images of childhood have also been constructed by historians, sociologists, anthropologists, and philosophers. Hobbes (1660) describes children as barbarians, as little devils beset by original sin. A hundred years later, Rousseau talks of 'little angels – children of nature' (1991). At the end of the nineteenth century, concerns about delinquent children led Key to propose that the twentieth century should become 'the century of the child' (1900), reflecting both the view that children should be taken seriously and the view that they needed help, as well as suggesting that parents might need state help with parenting. Reforming measures in the 1908 Children Act, such as the creation of Borstals, were set up because of anxiety about what children could become. As recently as 2000, Prout voices the same dualism: children in danger or children as dangerous.

Through the ages, then, children are depicted as wicked, innocent, angelic, subservient, victimised, etc. Hendrick (1997) tracks such changing images chronologically – starting with the natural child, the Romantic child, the evangelical child, the factory child, the delinquent child, the schooled child, and ending with the psychomedical child. While, as Thomas (2002) points out, such stereotypical images do not necessarily reflect the totality of conceptions of childhood at any one point in time (he suggests there is continuity over the ages in how parents valued and treated their children – certainly up to the age of seven, after which many were originally in employment, and are now in school), many of our adult attitudes today reflect the images described above and are carried with us in our treatment of children.

Adult attitudes to children today

Today, adult attitudes to children and what childhood comprises continue to be complex, ambivalent and often contradictory. In a recent survey undertaken by the Children's Society, *The Good Childhood:*

Searching for Values in a Competitive Age (2009), children are seen as both vulnerable and in need of protection, and as a threat to society. The view that children are both vulnerable, so need protection, and threatening, so need controlling are reflected in contradictory attitudes to the impact of recent social developments, such as information technology (IT) and commercialism.

INFORMATION TECHNOLOGY

Most young people in the UK today have a sophisticated understanding of communication technology; 64 per cent of children aged 8–15 have access to the internet at home and 65 per cent have a mobile phone. While their opportunities for information and communication are enhanced and can be exploited to advantage, power issues are raised for both parents and professionals. For parents, issues of supervision arise because of the dangers of pornography, website grooming and bullying. Parents need to monitor and ensure the safety of their children's use of technology and websites while they must also support their advantages for learning, communication, etc.

Social workers can also use computers to advantage to communicate with children – especially if they have a laptop to take into the children's homes. However, using technology can bring changes to relationships and interactions which may be problematic when dealing with vulnerable children, where face-to-face contact is needed to establish a relationship of trust. In comparing computer-based interviewing of children for assessments with face-to-face interviewing, Connolly (2005) found that direct face-to-face interviewing elicited more statements, encouraged more problems to be selected and captured a wider range of spontaneous responses than the computer-assisted interviewing. He concluded that, although children liked using computers and computer-based games could build up rapport, they did not replace the need for direct communication with professionals.

COMMERCIALISM

While the concept of children as consumers has fed the move to see children as social actors, and so having a right to have a voice, there are also concerns about risk and harm. The Compass Report (2006) suggested that adverts pressure children to grow up too soon and that they are groomed for consumerism by marketing that targets them directly, such as with images of what they should look like and own.

Again, tensions and differences can be created between what adults and children value and want, and the degree to which parents need to supervise and manage or control problematic consumer influences on their children.

The dilemmas created by technology and commercialism can thus create complex issues of power and control as well as secrecy between parents and children which are potentially dangerous. It can also reinforce a 'them and us' dynamic which is not conducive to engagement or power sharing.

BOUNDARIES BETWEEN CHILDHOOD AND ADULTHOOD

Another effect of social change is to make transitions from childhood to adolescence and from adolescence to adulthood less clear cut and more complex, with children becoming teenagers earlier and adults later. Schorr (1991) suggested that one effect of the shifting boundaries between childhood and adulthood is to set up cultures of contempt. While young people see themselves as different to adults, as being 'cool', oppositional and rebellious, half of the 2000 adults interviewed by YouGov for Barnardo's (Barnardo's 2008), thought children posed a danger to society, and 54 per cent that young people are 'beginning to behave like animals'. Although they believed that young people commit up to half of all crimes, in fact they are only responsible for 12 per cent. Such a perspective will not encourage adults to listen to or be respectful of children's views.

The influence of adult attitudes on children's views

Adult attitudes are, as suggested above, an important determinant of children's views, attitudes and behaviour. Research on the views of the children themselves also demonstrate contradictory responses. In surveying the views of 8000 young people, the Children's Society (2006) reported that young people valued the quality of relationships, they had concerns about safety and they wanted freedom in what they think, say and do. Similar findings were reported by the Children's Commissioner in Wales (2009). The 11,000 children interviewed there valued love and respect, safety and freedom. Of importance to them were family, friends, leisure, school, behaviour, local environment and money.

However, the Barnardo's YouGov survey reported above presented a contrary view: one in ten of the children said their life was not worth living. The Children's Society Reports (2006, 2009) provide evidence that, despite greater affluence, children's lives in all social classes are today more difficult. Since 2000, one in six children in the UK suffers from serious emotional or behavioural problems compared with only one in ten 15 years ago. Stress is produced by what is termed 'excessive individualism', which has impinged directly on children and also encourages rivalries. Many children are themselves struggling.

While the media does focus on dramatic images, there is evidence that negative and demonising attitudes exist. The Children's Commissioner in Wales (2009) identified cultural factors of individualism and materialism as proving disastrous for parenting as children become increasingly socially excluded by the anti-social behaviour agenda. And, of course, practitioners are not exempt both from imbibing such attitudes themselves, nor from being seen differently by children. Their attempts, and those of their employers, to involve children in participatory practice are affected by this history and by the currency in which they live.

DO YOUNG PEOPLE WANT TO PARTICIPATE?

While the UNCRC implies that all children want a high degree of citizenship and involvement in decision making at a number of levels, can that view be supported by their subsequent experiences? A study carried out by the Institute for Public Policy Research in 2002 reported that young people were enthusiastic about playing a part in decision-making processes at local level. Common issues were crime, personal safety, education, the environment and housing. A more recent evaluation of young people's participation in two Children's Trusts in England (National Youth Agency 2009) also found that they demonstrated high levels of commitment to involvement in decision making within the Trusts, for example through the use of web-based media, and by developing a network of Hear by Right Participation Champions involving all Trust partner agencies. Generally young people were more likely to participate in everyday life contexts such as youth projects. However, they felt schools weren't interested in young people's views. Few young people were aware of the UNCRC, and although it was difficult to find examples where young people's participation had a direct impact on outcomes, in terms of benefits for themselves the young people felt valued and respected for their contributions.

The influence of adult attitudes on professional approaches

Social attitudes to children and young people are reflected in some of the tensions and dilemmas that confront professionals, such as teachers and lawyers as well as social workers, in their work with children. Although New Labour placed children at the heart of the *Every Child Matters* agenda, this does not ensure that services are child centred or that children should be taken seriously. Brandon *et al.* (2008) talk of 'agency neglect' in relation to the high numbers of adolescent children with multiple difficulties who are not receiving services, reflecting, among other things, disjunctive attitudes to young people who are more likely to be regarded as troublesome than troubled.

EDUCATION

Similarly, in education, New Labour's key site for enhancing a sense of responsibility, citizenship and independence in young people – all factors clearly associated with the capacity to seek rights – there are split attitudes. The Good Childhood Inquiry (2009) suggests that the current focus on results in academic tests has been at the cost of promoting emotional wellbeing at critical life stages. Added to this, critiques of *Every Child Matters* suggest that while the five outcomes to be attained are strong on protection, recognition of needs and staying out of trouble, they are less forthcoming on how to create a culture of respect. There are some references to children's consultation in setting out outcomes, especially safety, but enjoying is hardly spelt out at all. This implies that getting through exams and keeping out of trouble is the most important outcome to achieve, setting a value base which is not necessarily 'in sync' with a participation agenda which values respect and encourages children to have a voice.

The recent controversy at the National Teachers Conference over the involvement of young people in teaching staff appointments in schools is further evidence of mixed attitudes to the participation agenda in schools. While government guidance, *Working Together: Listening to the Voices of Children and Young People* (DCSF 2008a), lays out the value of including pupils in staff appointments, the experience of some schools has been negative. They reported that the young people asked inappropriate questions, such as what was the applicant's favourite pop music? Recent focus groups with children (Davey 2010) suggest that children are more likely to be asked about food in the canteen and equipment in the playground than decisions about staff appointments and school budgets.

LOOKED-AFTER CHILDREN

Similarly, in residential units for young people, while some staff favour involving the young people in a range of decisions about the running of the unit – such as bed and meal times, available facilities and so on – others do not. This is despite the National Minimum Standards for Children in Care (Department of Health 2002b) which requires that 'the views of children…are taken into account in the development of necessary changes in the operation of the home' (p.22).

THE LEGAL SYSTEM

Divided attitudes continue to be reflected in the UK legal system. For example, 10-year-olds still have criminal responsibility, but cannot own a pet. The debate over raising the age of criminal responsibility, from 10 to 14, continues in spite of concerns over the criminalisation of the two 10-year-old boys convicted of the murder of James Bulger in 1982. Significantly, the question – were they victims or villains, in need of care or to be controlled? – continues to be asked today, nearly 30 years later, intensified by the re-offending on release in 2010 of one of the offenders, Robert Thompson.

The language in youth justice provides another example of the gap between care and control:

> …the substitution of the term justice by offending is symbolically vital. Such a shift represents deeper ideological and conceptual currents which have steadily gathered momentum…and within which children in trouble have increasingly been regarded, and thus treated, as offenders first and children second, if at all. (Goldson 2000, p.256)

The questions raised continue to be: do we treat and cure offending behaviour, or do we control and punish the offenders? Are they offenders first and children second? Are we talking about children in need, or children in trouble?

The effect of such attitudes on children's capacity to participate in court has been previously discussed with reference to their representation in court. Currently, in care or adoption proceedings, the children's views are generally presented by an advocate – a Children's Guardian from CAFCASS. While some judges are endeavouring to move to a position where the children can speak for themselves, others believe that they should be protected, are immature, are incompetent and should be represented by an adult.

The influence of adult attitudes on policy

A glance at changing legislation for children also reflects the contradictory constructions of childhood described above. Fox Harding (1991) identified four predominant perspectives informing English law over the last hundred years, from the *laissez faire* approach, where parents are left to bring up their children themselves, to state paternalism, where professionals are seen as protecting children, including from their parents. More recently the legislative shift has been to support parents' rights and children's rights, with the state supporting and working in partnership with parents and children. And children's autonomy is recognised.

However, all four perspectives can be traced through recent legislation, including the Children Act (1989), suggesting that the tensions underpinning these differing perspectives remain unresolved. In the UK New Labour's policies strongly reflect the conception of childhood as preparation for adulthood. *Every Child Matters*, reflecting Locke's seventeenth-century image of childhood touched on earlier, perceives children as citizens of the future, with good citizenship to be achieved by education and good training and by anti-poverty measures. However, despite the voice that children now have in policy, legislation cannot ensure either that all children are represented or that adults listen to what they say if they don't want to hear it. The recent Participation Works (Davey 2010) report describes some organisations as having 'adult-centric' ideas about the types of issues children should have a say in and reports that only some children are involved.

The influence of adult attitudes on research with children

Research approaches and methodologies also reflect shifts in adult attitudes to and theories of childhood, as illustrated by Darbyshire's work. He argued in 2000 that much research focusing on children's experiences was 'research on' rather than 'research with' or 'research for' children. However, following the Economic and Social Research Council's (ESRC) 'Children 5–16 Programme: Growing into the Twenty-First Century', he comments, five years later, upon the 'profound effect' on research related to children (Darbyshire, MacDougall and Schiller 2005).

The ESRC project comprised 22 linked research projects reviewing different aspects of children's lives, looking at 'children as social actors influencing as well as being influenced by their environment' (Darbyshire, MacDougall and Schiller 2005, p.420). According to Prout (2002) 'including children as research subjects, rather than objects of enquiry, has been shown to reveal many novel aspects of the situations, settings and issues they were asked about' (p.68). Morrow (2001) has also written about the impact on research and on research methodologies of the transformation of the child from a project to a person. This will be explored in more detail in the research studies presented in Part II.

Adult attitudes to children and to children's rights thus clearly influence the degree to which, and the arenas in which, children are encouraged and helped to participate. I turn now to another global influence on children's opportunities to participate: the world in which they live.

Social disadvantage

The world in which children live is an important factor in enabling children and young people to take up the participatory rights accorded to them by law. Their living environment is crucial in affecting both their own capacities and the opportunities that are open to them, as well as the time and resources available to their social workers. Poverty and abuse, as well as factors linked to demography and health, can combine to create structural and emotional barriers to participatory practice both at individual and organisational levels.

Children's rights in developed countries are reduced when they are disadvantaged by the following factors:

* poverty, debt, worklessness and low aspirations
* low parental education and skills

- domestic violence
- relationship conflict
- child neglect and poor parenting and family functioning
- poor mental health
- poor physical health and disabilities
- teenage pregnancy
- learning disability
- poor school attendance and attainment
- involvement in crime, anti-social behaviour and substance misuse
- poor housing and homelessness.

(DCSF 2010, pp.287–288)

Poverty

Bradshaw's report for the UN (2006) and the later UNICEF (2007a) report on childhood in industrialised countries both provide strong evidence that poverty harms children and so can be regarded as a violation of children's rights and create barriers to their participation. The UK had the fifth highest child poverty rate and the highest proportion of children living in workless families in the European Union. A report of 2000 young people from workless households (The Prince's Trust 2007) shows that they are much less positive about the future than those from families where the parents are in employment, and that they lack confidence and basic skills, such as time keeping. Clearly this will impact adversely upon their capacity to become involved in decision-making forums.

Child poverty is also concentrated geographically, so it is higher, for example, in parts of Wales. Research conducted in Bristol by Cuthbert and Hatch (2008) highlighted that in certain kinds of communities, covering two million households, the levels of aspiration among young people are 10 per cent below the national average. This gap is typically found in northern cities where there are large numbers of families on benefits and high rates of social housing. These communities are predominantly white working class and insular in that there is little community activity. Such factors compound in reducing both young people's capacity for and opportunities to participate in organisational issues.

Another factor affecting the capacity of children from disadvantaged homes and locations to engage in participatory practice, perhaps especially in influencing organisational change, is their access to technology. The Digital Exclusion Task Force (2009) found that in 2007 the UK ranked eighteenth in the world in connectivity, with only 661 out of every 1000 people connected. They hypothesised that those who weren't connected were in the socially excluded groups. Given that many of the children in need are in disadvantaged and socially excluded groups, this will need to be taken into account in determining children's ability to work on computers with their social workers. This will be discussed later in this book, in Chapter 8.

Demographic change

Poverty is also more prevalent in certain types of household, such as large families (43% of poor children live in large families), and in families where the mother is aged under 25. In Bradshaw's study one in four children in the UK had experienced parental separation, one in four was born to a lone parent and one in four remained an only child. Frost and Featherstone (2003) also provide evidence of the ways in which recent demographic changes such as delayed fertility, falling birth rates and the relative instability of new family forms impacts upon children's experiences, the social space in which they live and the opportunities open to them to be involved in decision-making arenas.

Education and health

Educational achievement and good health, key to children's capacity to participate, are also dependent on parental income and support. In tracking two cohorts from birth to aged 30, Hobcroft (2007) found that educational test scores and poverty were statistically significant for all, and that health also had a pervasive effect.

Links have also been established between household income and mental health problems. Health in the UK has not improved in the last five years. There is an increased risk of parental depression, which impacts in a variety of ways on the health and welfare of children in the family and so on their capacity to engage in their social work and participate in decisions that are made about their care. Some children,

for example, will find it extremely difficult to get to .
express their wishes because they are looking after siblings
for a depressed mother (see Aldridge and Becker 2003).

Children and young people in the UK have a higher incide.
of mental and physical ill health than children from other European
countries. Additionally, Graham (2008) found that rates of depression,
anxiety and mental health in children were higher in poor households
(Bennett 2008). Those who are ill, are physically disabled or have
learning needs face very particular problems in participating, as
previously described.

The impact of poverty, disadvantage and abuse on participatory practice

Here I would like to group together the combined impacts from poverty,
disadvantage and abuse, first on children's capacity to participate, and
second on the professional's abilities to promote it.

THE IMPACT ON THE CHILDREN

Jack and Gil (2010) suggest that the public distrust of child protection
professionals engendered in poor communities has the following
effects:

- It deters the families from using services.

- It means that information about services is unavailable.

- It means that there are differing cultural expectations around issues
  of confidentiality, consultation and partnership.

They go on to point out that the adult's suspicion and the lack of
engagement engendered by the involvement of professionals is picked
up by the children. A 12-year-old boy, interviewed in Chapter 7 about
his experience of being involved in a child protection conference
expresses this view well:

> 'What I would like most would be for them [the social workers] not to
> come and see us any more and let us get on with our lives.'

This boy's negative response is very likely to reflect that of his carers
and can also contribute to setting up defence mechanisms, such as
denial, to avoid conflict (see Schofield and Thoburn 1996). In families
that are violent many children will go to great lengths to hide the

existence of violence because they fear the consequences of telling. They may also have learned that adults do not want to hear. For children from minority ethnic communities, concepts such as family honour can prevent children from disclosing as well as stopping their mothers from reporting risk and conflict in the home.

Another aspect of the negative influence of environment and social disadvantage on children's ability to participate is described by Howe (1995). He points out that the more adverse a child's social environment is or has been, the more difficult it will be for that child to develop a coherent sense of self – and so to be involved in decisions about his care. Ryan, Wilson and Fisher (1995) provide a good example of this in their discussion of therapeutic work with children who are looked after. In working toward enabling young people in foster care to express their views about who they would like to live with or have contact with Ryan *et al.* write, 'It is only when the child is in a secure and supportive situation that he/she may be free to address earlier trauma' (p.133).

THE IMPACT ON THEIR SOCIAL WORKERS

Social workers working to facilitate children and young people's involvement in decision-making forums in disadvantaged communities thus face a 'double whammy'. Not only do they need to understand and address the negative influence of environment and social disadvantage on the children they are working with. In disadvantaged areas they have additional problems.

These include the following:

- The resources the practitioners have on the ground to facilitate children's involvement may be limited and the facilities poor.

- The practical difficulties – for example, enabling a young person to attend a meeting – are likely to be much greater where the young people and their parents have no money. Venue, time and transport can be especially important in helping younger children to get to meetings – but require more of the social worker's time to arrange and carry out.

- Ensuring poor families have all their welfare entitlements may rate higher as a priority than talking to the child.

- Levels of crime and violence may be high and so discourage the sorts of community engagement which would encourage children and young people to participate, and discourage social workers from visiting them at home.

- Case loads are likely to be high, so the time available to spend in direct work is more limited.

TIME AND RESOURCES

The importance of time in engaging children in participatory practice cannot be over-stressed. In working with children who are socially excluded or experiencing these sorts of disadvantage, the establishment of trust over time is essential. Kohli (2006) found that it could take years for young, unaccompanied asylum seekers to trust workers enough to speak to them. Ward (2008) and Schofield (2005) also describe the length of time it takes for young people in care to understand what is happening, to manage conflicting loyalties and to be able to speak freely about their wishes and feelings.

In an evaluation based on a postal survey of local authority child care managers, Thomas (2005) reported that the most common obstacles to the inclusion of children in decision making were practitioners' lack of time due to high case loads, and the demands of complex child care cases, court reports and care assessments. More recently, this was also recognised by the Social Work Task Force (2009, p.7) following the Peter Connelly Review: 'social workers need some immediate action to improve their day to day working expertise'. The shortage of resources, such as available day care, and of the time necessary to support work with problem families, makes empowering practice with their children more difficult to achieve.

SECRECY AND FEAR

Where levels of crime and violence are high, parents who do not want their child to be heard or to participate in the decision-making process can provide a plethora of physical and psychological barriers which can be extremely difficult to penetrate. Secrecy and fear permeate violent families, silence the children and frighten the professionals who endeavour to make contact (Bell 2002; Garboden 2010). Families where there is violence arouse feelings of helplessness and fear in those who are there to help which are deskilling and disempowering. The practitioner's experiences of disempowerment may well mirror those of the children involved who are also silenced or use strategies of denial or avoidance to manage fear and keep safe.

A number of research studies on children who have witnessed domestic violence (see Hester, Pearson and Harwin 2007) evidence the children's reticence to talk about it for fear of increased risk to themselves, to others in the family, or of the perpetrator's removal from home. Similarly children experiencing or witnessing bullying at school fear to disclose it in case of retribution (Ofsted 2003).

Such dynamics, highlighted in public inquiries and serious case reviews (Brandon *et al.* 2008), explain the lack of power practitioners face themselves in working with abusive families. This was illustrated by the social worker in the Climbié case who was obstructed from seeing the child by the dominant aunt. Similarly, with Peter Connelly, the child's mother prevented access to the male partner who murdered her baby. And with Khyra Ishaq, aged 7, who died of starvation in 2009: although she had been removed from school two years earlier for home tuition, social workers had not insisted on seeing her, partly because of the mother's antagonism (see Birmingham Safeguarding Children Board 2010).

A recurring theme of successive public inquiries into abuse has been the failure to listen to children. What these public inquiries, and the subsequent serious case reviews, draw to our attention are some of the barriers that get in the way of talking and listening to children, and thus the need for social workers to take into account a range of environmental, personal, cultural and family relationship factors when helping children to have a voice in child protection work.

Organisational change, culture and practice

The last factor impacting upon the professional's capacity to engage in participatory practice with children to consider here is the organisations that employ them. In Children's Departments and other agencies, the structures and processes which enable practitioners and motivate children to be involved need to be in place. Initially progress was slow. The Robbins Report (Robbins 2001) found that many authorities were starting from a long way back, and three years later a report entitled *Listen Then Commission* (Fry 2003) found that only a few young people in the authorities they surveyed had been actively involved in the recruitment and training of foster carers, for example, although they felt they had much to contribute.

The current picture is more positive. Participation Works (Davey 2010) reports on considerable investment in resources, training and events, with more organisations having a dedicated participation worker and a champion for participation. However, they found that senior staff were less likely to be trained or involved and that practices were not embedded in all levels because the approach was 'bottom up'.

Clearly, participation at a number of different levels requires organisations to change – to change their ethos and culture, and to change at all levels: senior management, frontline staff, and across both policy and practice. Different levels of participation will depend upon the organisation's stage of development. Kirby *et al.*'s (2003) study highlights ways in which organisations can start to build cultures of participation. It draws on research from 29 case studies indicating the ways in which organisations have moved across levels: from being consultation-focused to participation-focused to child-focused.

Wright and Haydon (2002) have suggested that participatory practice in organisations can be progressed by establishing a commitment to participation, planning and developing participatory ways of working and building up the skills, knowledge and experience required by practitioners and by the young people themselves. Chapter 9 provides a good illustration of how one authority set about creating and developing ways of feeding children's views about their services back into their policy decision making, and what systems within the organisation facilitated this or got in the way.

However, while there have been a raft of initiatives and developments intended to support children's participation in social work, and these practice developments have and are continuing, there has also been an increasing emphasis in Children's Departments on tight procedural detail and managerialism enforced by New Labour and following the Laming Reports 2003 and 2009. One of the impacts of the massive organisational changes that have ensued, of relevance here, is on the culture of social work practice in so far as the participation of children in it is concerned.

Managerialism

Lonne *et al.* (2008) talk of a 'case management' culture where professional discretion has been replaced by complex procedural guidance focusing on quality control, targets and performance indicators. One effect on Children's Departments is the increase in administrative work, meaning less time for relationship-based work. The research reported in Chapter 8 shows how the shift to electronic recording systems, for example, has reduced the time practitioners spend in direct work with children (Bell *et al.* 2007). Another effect is on reducing the professional's sense of expertise and confidence, essential to engaging children in difficult child protection work.

Munro (2005) and Garrett (2005) decry that managerialism has taken priority over the direct and time-consuming work that is needed to promote the participation of vulnerable young people. So the tensions outlined here, between supporting a culture which has as its dominant value base the human rights of children but is also promoting the values of business efficiency, remain unresolved. And they get in the way of promoting children's participatory rights.

This chapter ends Part I, which has provided the context and theoretical and policy background to the increasing involvement of children and young people in a range of decision-making arenas. Part II provides illustrative accounts of children's experiences of participation in their social work by describing four research studies carried out between 2000 and 2008. It ends by pulling out the implications for practice.

PART II

Research Studies on Children's Experiences of Participation

Introduction

Having defined what participation means, discussed the policy and theoretical background and explored what might promote it and what might get in the way, I now turn to fleshing out in more detail some arenas in social work in which children have participated. In this part of the book, the next four chapters describe research studies on the involvement of children in different situations, from those where children were personally involved in social work interventions – child protection, family group conferences and electronic record systems – to one reporting on their participation in service planning and delivery in one local authority.

There is now a substantive literature on children's views of services they use and other types of interventions in which they take part. Examples from the existing research literature on their involvement in their social work include: Shemmings (2000) and Sanders and Mace (2006) on child protection conferences; Holland (2006) on family group conferences, and on looked-after children (2010); Kohli (2006) on unaccompanied asylum-seeking children; Morris (1999) on disabled children's views of their placements; Munro (2001) and McLeod (2010) on looked-after children's views; Carroll (2002) on children's views of play therapy.

There is also a growing body of research on children's experiences of their family lives, such as Smart et al. (2001) and Butler et al. (2002) on children's views on divorce. On service provision, children's experience of Private Law Court Proceedings was researched by the NSPCC (2007), and Triangle/NSPCC (2001, 2002) explored disabled children's views on residential respite centres and health and education services.

And there are studies of children's views on advocacy (Ofsted 2008; Barnes 2007); on children's participation in research (Murray 2003); and on their involvement in organisational issues (Cairns and Brannen 2005; Davey 2010).

Research methodologies

A number of research methodologies have been used to elicit the views of children. As reviewed by Hill (1997) these include observation; self completion questionnaires; individual interviews; focus groups; use of vignettes; written and/or pictorial prompts; drawing; role play and the use of technical aids. Generally, quantitative measures such as rating scales are not as effective in gaining children's views as qualitative methods, such as semi-structured interviews. However, quantitative research is important in enabling trends and commonalities to be determined. Many children can complete questionnaires on their own, including on-line. The value of obtaining numbers of completed questionnaire responses is illustrated in Chapter 9, where 76 children completed questionnaires, providing a comprehensive account of their views on their experiences of social work and on their involvement in service planning.

The research described in Chapter 9 illustrates the value of combining the two methods of collecting data. The questionnaires were followed up by a focus group with the children and by a small number of detailed interviews giving in-depth and detailed narrative accounts of their experiences. Qualitative research, such as this, enabled a more nuanced and detailed response to be gained and, as this study demonstrates, both methods of collecting children's views can be used at the same time. Hill (2006) and O'Kane (2002) pick up on issues of power imbalance in qualitative research, and suggest this can be addressed by offering children choices, such as of where to meet, to opt out at any stage, to have a supporter and so on.

Some researchers, such as Hogan (1997), advocate the use of unstructured questioning when interviewing children, arguing that this allows children to clarify their thinking and provides more accurate, comprehensible reports of their experiences. Aubrey and Dahl's (2006) review concluded that effective strategies used to engage children under the age of 12 were those which included the use of enactment, props, drawing and computer-based approaches (e.g. Clark 2004). Rewards for the time taken, such as book tokens, can reinforce for children the value of their contribution. The children in Chapter 7 who were interviewed about their involvement in child protection conferences and reviews were given the choice of a gift voucher, donated by local shops. In Chapter 9, describing children's participation in the local authority survey, pizzas and drinks were made available at the focus groups.

Researching the perspectives of children with disabilities poses other challenges. Mitchell *et al.* (2009) point out the importance of time in interviewing disabled children, especially when working with young people with learning disabilities or non-verbal communication. Developing rapport with them and talking to them is a slow process. In their research, the use of different tools, such as the Talking Mats, card-based tasks and British Sign Language (BSL) communication, which provided data that differed from that produced by more traditional verbal semi-structured interviews, is illustrated. While the BSL-based data was as rich as data produced by the spoken word, the symbol-based data provided invaluable insights about the lives and priorities of two previously marginalised groups. Mitchell also used symbols in talking to the children in the Integrated Children's System study described in Chapter 8. These research experiences demonstrate the need to move beyond and challenge traditional ideas of what is deemed 'appropriate' and acceptable knowledge (see also Nolan *et al.* 2007). They also emphasise the need for skilled and effective communicators.

Where research is set up to explore sensitive, personal issues, such as in child protection or divorce, a number of management issues arise. It is crucial to gain the child's consent, and decisions need to be made as to the capacity of the child to know what they are consenting to and whether the parents should also be asked to give consent. In the case of looked-after children the matter is complicated further because the local authority stands *in loco parentis*. In the research described in Chapter 7 on interviewing children about their experiences of child protection investigations a steering group consisting of professionals from the Area Child Protection Committee advised on issues of consent, confidentiality and follow-up.

Gatekeeping issues are properly raised, especially with groups of children who are perceived to be emotionally vulnerable, and after-care support needs to be provided where necessary. Strickland-Clarke, Campbell and Dallos (2000), for example, report family therapists as being concerned about the disruptive or unsettling effects of interviewing children. Jäger (2009) points out that this 'professional concern' may be compounded when the child attending therapy is also a child who is looked after by the local authority. Indeed, all local authorities now have their own governance schemes, requiring researchers to gain permission before carrying out any research with children in their care. Where they are also in receipt of health services, NHS ethics committee procedures serve to protect children's safety and anonymity. And it is important to ensure the children participating know confidentiality is assured, have feedback and see the outcome of their contribution. The children interviewed in the family group conference research described in Chapter 6 were sent a leaflet outlining the main findings of the study, and what the recommendations to the local authority comprised.

Researchers are also now using reference groups to inform their research methodologies, and an example of this is that used in the Integrated Children's System study in Chapter 8. Here focus groups of young people were set up to enable decisions to be made about the most effective way of communicating with the young service users. To ensure our research interviews were child friendly and to get pointers for the semi-structured questionnaires, we consulted with a group of young people accessed through a local Children's Rights Project. Two focus groups were set up, one for 10–14-year-olds and one for over 14s.

The under-14s focus group was based on a series of activities designed to engage the young people. The activities were constructed to encourage their reflection on communication with professionals. This included a role play of an award ceremony for the best and worst social worker, and a game where the children ran to opposite ends of the room depending on whether they agreed or disagreed with statements about social workers and social work practice. A key theme of this session, reflecting the findings reported in previous chapters, was that the personality and attention given to them as individuals by social workers was the most important aspect of their contact.

The session with those aged over 14 was held in their weekly drama club meeting, following advice that this group were used to expressing themselves through drama. The session comprised a short sketch, with the brief to construct a short drama presentation about 'being interviewed'. The first sketch was based around a formal impersonal interview to join the Army. In contrast, the group in the second sketch depicted a caring and attentive interviewer.

The difference between the two age groups was striking. While the over-14s were more reflective about their experiences, be it of care or of child protection procedures, the younger ones were more comfortable discussing their experience in an interview and found the experience helpful in enabling them to rethink difficult times and to unlock emotions.

The research studies that follow

In the next four chapters the methodology used to explore the experiences of children of different ages and of differing abilities is described so that the findings can be set in the context of the methods used. In all four studies a number of the children were interviewed by use of a semi-structured questionnaire, in one case supplemented by a focus group of young people. In two, questionnaires were used to gain more basic factual information, such as whether or not the children had attended a review, and to provide some quantitative data to support the qualitative data obtained in the interviews. To gain the views of the professionals involved interviews were also undertaken with the children's social workers and, where relevant, with their managers.

Detailed leaflets were produced initially so that the children knew what the research was about and they all signed consent forms. Ethics permission was gained from the ethics committees of the relevant departments, and in every case a steering group advised on progress. To acknowledge the time the children committed to each project they were given a gift voucher and a child-friendly resumé of the findings at the end.

CHAPTER 6

The Involvement of Children in Family Group Conferences

'You don't really talk at home like we did there, at the meeting…we are quite a close family but because it's a drug habit, you tiptoe round it…but when we were there, it was only about that, so you have to talk about it. So brilliant, great – we didn't feel like you had to hold anything back, you could just talk freely…' (15-year-old girl, who had been using drugs)

In this chapter, the participation of children in family group conferences is explored with reference to a study (Bell and Wilson 2002, 2006) to evaluate the first year of a family group conferences pilot project. The aims were to establish whether or not family group conferences were successful in increasing children's sense of engagement in a meeting which, unlike initial child protection conferences and review meetings, is not dominated by professionals and which sets out to enable families to work together to find their own way of managing their problems.

Family group conferences (FGCs) originated in New Zealand as a more radical way of working with families with children in need. The essence of a family group conference is that where there are concerns about a child's welfare or safety, the extended family is brought together to consider the child's welfare, to engage in detailed negotiation among themselves, and if possible to construct a plan of action which the family members and the professionals feel confident will help to secure the child's wellbeing.

A FGC is a decision making and planning process whereby the wider family group makes plans and decisions for the children and young people who have been identified either by the family or by service providers as being in need of a plan that will safeguard and promote their welfare. (DCSF 2010, p.284)

Although there is no legal requirement to use FGCs in England and Wales, a majority of local authorities offer them to families on a range of welfare issues (Family Rights Group 2008). They are not thought to be appropriate for use in the child protection decision-making process. The most recent guidance, *Working Together* (DCSF 2010) re-emphasises their role in implementing the principles of working in partnership, and it stresses the importance for children of maintaining links with their families. It states that:

> Family group conference may be appropriate in a number of contexts where there is a plan or decision to be made…they may be valuable, for example for children in need where a plan is required for the child's future welfare…and where, following Section 47 enquiries, support services are required. (p.284)

FGCs are seen as providing a means for more effectively involving the extended family, to have a particular role in keeping children out of care and as a way of working in partnership with families by locating power in the family unit rather than in the professional domain. Holland (2006) suggests that this method has the potential to shift the balance of power from the state while, at the same time, democratising decision making within families. Including children in the decision-making process is seen as supporting the rights of children to be involved in decisions that affect them – and so in line with the participatory agenda.

Key stages in the process are: careful preparation of the children and families by the professionals beforehand; the giving of information and setting out of the reasons for the meeting by the professionals at its outset; private time when the family reviews possibilities among themselves and considers what support from family members or social service might be needed; and finally the development, if possible, of a plan to which all can agree. A convener is on hand for the family and an advocate may be appointed to help the children or other family members voice their views.

As far as the children's participation is concerned, as in other meetings, careful preparation, good planning and the use of a support person or advocate can facilitate it. A crucial question is how or whether children can be involved in the process of decision making and planning to achieve change in a way which is empowering to them.

The study

The study that follows, of 25 FGCs undertaken in the north of England in 2000, will address a number of these issues. The FGC project entailed a partnership between the local authority and Barnardo's in the context of refocusing children's services and of implementing a child care strategy which aimed at developing more support and prevention in the city, as well as maximising partnership working with children in need. The study aimed to establish whether, among other things, the family group conference model was successful in increasing the commitment of children to planning and their engagement in the process.

Method

Referral information and copies of all the FGC plans were collected on the first 20 cases which reached conference. Conveners completed a questionnaire at the end of each FGC, giving basic information on the family attending, timing, length of private time, plans and resources agreed, and their rating of the likelihood of the plan's success. The views of children and adult family members in attendance were collected by a brief questionnaire, completed at the end of the conference, and by follow-up interviews at home in the weeks following the FGC. Following the conference, telephone interviews were also held with the case holder or social workers.

The sample
THE FAMILIES

The family members present at the 20 conferences researched included mothers/stepmothers and fathers/stepfathers and their partners, maternal and paternal grandparents and their partners, aunts, uncles, cousins and siblings. Grandparents were present in 13 of the conferences, and aunts or uncles in ten. In seven, friends of the family, including of the child, were present. Four conferences took place without mothers present, and eight without fathers or stepfathers.

THE CHILDREN

Thirty children were involved aged from 2 to 16. Most (53%) were aged between 10 and 14. Gender distribution was fairly even, there being 14 girls and 16 boys. In three of the families the children were subject to statutory orders: two on care orders and two on residence orders with their grandmother. Only one child was on the child protection register. Seventeen of the 30 children were present at the conference, 13 of whom were aged over 10. In one conference the school-age children had not been invited; in another the 14-year-old had attended for ten minutes, evidently as much as he could manage even with a supreme effort.

Fifteen children aged between 6 and 16 from nine FGCs completed questionnaires, of whom nine were later interviewed. Two of the questionnaires were from children who had not been in the conference room, but had played nearby. In eight conferences no responses from the children were received, either because they were too young (aged under 5) or had not been present.

THE FGCS

The average number of family members present in a FGC was 6.5, varying from the largest with 13 family members present (including three children), to the smallest, with only the mother and three children present. Their average length, including private time, was two hours 40 minutes and generally determined by the family. Since the social workers were rarely present the only others present for varying parts of the time were the conveners, and advocates. Advocates were present in three of the conferences as advocates for children, and in at least one, for a parent.

Findings
Reasons for holding the FGC

The most common reason was that the children's difficult behaviour was causing problems at home or at school. The intention was to enable the parents and children together to mobilise support from the wider family network to maintain the children's care at home or, less commonly, to enable a child accommodated by the local authority to be cared for within the family. In a number of cases the primary carers were the grandparents of the children, and the stress or ill health they were suffering meant they needed additional support to continue with their caring role. A feature of a minority of cases was that relationships with social services had broken down, and the plan was to enhance the family's sense of trust in social services by emphasising the role of the family in change.

Children's views

The questionnaires comprised straightforward questions about how comfortable and happy or sad they felt, their degree of understanding of what was happening, and whether they felt they could say everything they wanted (see Table 6.1).

The questionnaire responses suggest a predominantly favourable view of the conferences. The children appreciated the practical efforts made to make them feel welcome – food and drink was the item most frequently mentioned, followed by seeing members of their family and the chance for the family to talk. Dislikes were relatively few, except for the child whose conference had clearly not been a good experience, who wrote that she disliked 'everything'.

The interviews covered similar questions to the questionnaire, and further validated those findings. The children's experiences of the FGC were predominantly favourable, stressing the practical efforts made to make them feel welcome, seeing members of their family and the chance for the family to talk.

Table 6.1 Children's satisfaction ratings of the conference

	Yes	No	
I could say all I wanted	11	2	
I understood what was being said	12	1	
I felt comfortable	10	2	
Some things made me sad	5	8	
It was a good idea to have a conference	10	2	
Was someone there to speak for you?	11	1	
	Very	Quite	Not
How happy about the conference	11	3	1
How happy about the plans	9	4	2
How happy about who came	15		

Note: numbers do not always add up to the same total because each child did not answer every question.

Purpose of the meeting

All save one 6-year-old had a clear idea of what the meeting was for, with the older ones able to be quite specific. The reasons they gave tally with the identified purposes of the FGC: to mobilise family support – 'where I was going to if my dad was ill' – or to address their own problem behaviour:

> 'If I was here [i.e. at home] just talking about it, I'd be a bit stroppy. Like, I go flippy and walk out. But in that environment, I can't – so it's to sort me out.'

> 'To understand my behaviour, and I have to behave and go to sleep at the right times and everything, and be good at school.'

The younger children were less clear about the purposes of the meeting, and focused on immediate benefits, such as 'a chocolate bar' or, more unrealistically, an outing to 'swimming, ice skating, pictures'.

Preparation for the meeting

Despite not having been consulted previously about who should be invited, generally the children knew who would be there:

> 'My nanna, my auntie, my dad, me and my sister.'

> 'I didn't think my nana would be there, but she was…[but] my mum didn't come.'

Some of the older children also had clear views about what would be discussed and what might happen. They wanted 'to have a very good discussion'. Several wanted to re-establish contact with an absent parent:

> 'To talk about supervised contact with my mum and to find out where I was going when my dad went into hospital.'

Where the concerns involved their behaviour there were more mixed feelings:

> 'All my bad behaviour and stuff. I didn't like it so I kicked off.'

Choice and advocacy

While most of the children had not expected to be given much say in what would happen and were unperturbed by the lack of choice, the older children were somewhat clearer, feeling they had been consulted, for example, about having an advocate. Of the four who had advocates, two found them helpful. One 13-year-old was specific that he had been asked and declined:

Boy: 'I said, no, I'd speak for myself.'

Researcher: 'And did you manage to speak for yourself?'

Boy: 'Yes.'

Another checked with his mother whether 'his speaker' had said anything. His mother said:

'Just certain things that S couldn't pronounce you know – get out for himself. He stood up for him and spoke for him.'

It was not always clear whether an advocate had been present. The children themselves were vague. In at least two cases where an advocate had been present, the children said this was not the case. Either they could not remember or they were unclear of their function. In one conference, which had been a negative experience for the young person, she could not recall being asked if she wanted someone there for her.

Experience of being in the conference

Most were unclear about being given any information before or at the beginning of the conference, although they agreed with the identified concerns. Memories of this part of the conference were, as is the case with child protection conferences, hazy. Likewise, their experience, overall, was mixed – for some it had been wholly positive, while others had experienced it as some good, some bad. Only one found it wholly bad. Two had been pleased about the care taken in the arrangements. All the children wished to be included in the private time.

POSITIVE EXPERIENCES

Some children felt safe and appreciated the presence of their family:

'Good, positive – I was very safe, comfortable, and I was very happy at that place. Plus I'd got the family as well. We really got on together except for Aunty Dot!' (13-year-old girl)

For the 15-year-old girl quoted at the beginning of this chapter, after living with her mother after two years in foster care, the FGC proved a turning point in her efforts to kick her drug habit. She was rejoining the access course that she had abandoned some months ago and was getting ready to go on the residential drug treatment programme. It was striking that the opportunity to talk in depth with the family at home had never happened, but was facilitated by the conference.

'I had the choice whether I wanted to go or not [in relation to joining the scheme] and all the family around me decided whether it was a good idea, and whether it was good for me. I think it was me that made the decisions really. So that's good, because I've never been able to do that before, I've just had social workers just making decisions for me, you know, without even consulting me, so that was really *brilliant*, because you get to decide yourself.'

Both this girl and her mum were glowing about the experience and the impact it had on their lives. The family live in a notoriously run-down district in the city, and were battle hardened from years of contact with social services and other agencies. They saw this process as separate and different from the statutory one, for here the convener was independent of social services:

'Someone with her feet on the ground – she's lovely – she's sound as a pound – she's really lived life – she was like me really.'

The preparation time, with the convener making two or three visits to the house, had helped to create a friendly, informal atmosphere and provided a chance for the family to get together to see what they themselves could come up with. In this case, this was successful. Four months afterwards the girl was surviving back home, needing support but still off drugs.

A view expressed by a number of the children, echoing the girl above, was that having a discussion with the family without the social workers present was valuable, if 'weird':

'Different. Because the social workers and all that lot weren't there.'

Another positive experience was of realising that the family cared about them, and sharing insight about the impact of their own behaviour on those close to them is illuminated by this 14-year-old girl:

'Even though they were just like my mum, my auntie and my sister tell you…you get to know how much they really are worrying. And how much they really do care. So you take a step back, and you think, well, I'm hurting them with what I'm doing.'

MIXED EXPERIENCES

Not all children felt comfortable with the intensity of the family feelings and discussion evoked in the conference. For one quite troubled 12-year-old boy, the conference had proved a mixed experience. Although he had been taken aback at the caring expressed by his grandparents, he felt awkward and embarrassed. At the same time he appreciated the longer-term benefits that had accrued and was able to take some responsibility for his own contribution to family problems:

> *Boy*: 'I didn't like it. I just didn't like everyone being together.'

> *Researcher*: 'Was there anything you liked?'

> *Boy*: 'I didn't know that my nana and granddad cared that much – I just didn't know.' [His mother interjects that they've told him before, and he adds 'But it was hearing it, hearing them saying it.']

> *Researcher*: 'Do you think things have changed for you at all since the meeting?'

> *Boy*: 'Yes, school. Something came out of it – I got my school back. I've been in – it works out about five or six times since.'

In another, the child said that she had been very sad about the plan that was made, but was eventually persuaded by the support worker that the plan was positive and helpful, and she finally changed her mind.

NEGATIVE EXPERIENCES

Only one 15-year-old girl, now pregnant and living with friends, had experienced the conference as almost entirely negative. Unlike the children above, who had found the absence of the social workers facilitating, she had felt abandoned when the convener and her social worker went out:

> 'It was just stupid, Sarah and Andrew [social worker and convener] walking out and leaving us. Because even though they are my aunties and uncles and that and I do know them you haven't seen them for ages and they're just throwing all these questions at you.'

A powerful aspect of her concern was that she felt she had been identified as the problem when, in her view, her mother was the real problem and she was the victim:

Girl: 'Really it was all about my mam. It was just "her mam isn't her mother is she?" And "her mam should have been here, her mam this and her mam that." And why did I do it. I was in bits after all that.'

Researcher: 'Did you think what they came up with was a good plan?'

Girl: 'No – because my uncle was going "I'd have her stop here at my house, but she's got a baby." And the plan included taking me out every Thursday – it's my day off school, so I didn't want to. And I couldn't have said "I don't want that" because I was like stuck in the middle.'

In this conference, a strength was that her grandmother said she would take her in if things became difficult elsewhere, and the 15-year-old felt that she could be trusted.

CHILDREN'S VIEWS ON OUTCOMES

Views were mixed as to what had improved, what remained unchanged and what made worse. A few thought nothing had changed, while most thought things had got better, and that they had had some influence. The comments highlight another issue which appeared central, and which other researchers have also identified – the importance of there being a follow-through from social services of what has been decided at the meeting. The following is from a 14-year-old girl with long experience of being looked after:

'It's not that we were sat there, we talked about it and after that jack all got done, because I bet in some cases that does happen. But in my case it was good – they were brilliant, the people they gave us, so if it wasn't for them, none of this would have happened anyway. They had a great understanding with us. They made us feel comfortable. They didn't make us feel like we had to watch what we said – we could speak how we spoke. It just depends who you get and whether your social worker can be bothered.'

Other positive comments included closer family relationships:

'We're a bit closer in understanding each other – well, in understanding me.'

Views of the meeting, overall, were that it was 'worth a try', 'a good way to sort things out', 'absolutely brilliant'.

However, not all children found the experience helpful. Returning to the 15-year-old girl with the drug problem who was quoted earlier, nothing had changed: 'I [left] feeling just mixed up.' She found the process wholly unhelpful and disempowering: 'They just stick you in a room to scrap.'

Carer's views on the presence of the children

While some thought it helpful that the children should hear everything, others did not:

> 'We had to be careful what we said because the children were there…'

Some parents expressed some sensitivity about the children's feelings, but this led to them avoiding discussion of key issues:

> 'We talked fine, but I didn't know what to say, really, and what really to ask for…I avoided talking about S's problems because I didn't want to label him.'

A small minority felt the FGC was 'over the top' and too tiring for the children:

> 'We could have had the meeting at home, it would have been cheaper, less public, easier.'

Clearly the issue of how private time is managed is crucial to the process and varied from one conference to another. It seemed in this study, unlike Holland's (2006), that the professionals exercised less rather than more control over the process and this was not always experienced as helpful by the families.

Social workers' views

Of the 19 social workers interviewed, all were enthusiastic in principle of the opportunity to work in partnership:

> 'It is a very useful tool – in the sense of working in partnership and empowering the people we work with.'

Having a means of relocating responsibility for change within the family itself was also welcomed:

> 'A good new way of working…puts the responsibility back with them.'

However, as with Holland's (2006) study, more caution was expressed about its application in practice, with a number wanting to wait and see, being prepared for it to work better with some families than others.

Reservations were expressed about power dynamics within families dominated by a particular member or group:

> 'I do have reservations. If there is too little family network support in there, and if there is a great dominance in there from one party, I think that [other] people's voices might not be heard, and they could be railroaded into a course of action…and I question how empowering that might be.'

The process of engaging and bringing the families together with the children was seen by many as offering a new opportunity to break down a negative pattern which had grown up between themselves and social services.

Outcomes

One task of the conference was to draw up a plan, which should contain details of the children's views, and be used as the basis for planning and review. This was usually left to the family members to devise and write and few seemed to be clear about what was in the plan. Some of the plans were excessively brief, and consisted largely of wish lists (for example, rooms decorated, bicycles for the children). Again, there is a tension here between enabling the adults and children to take ownership of the plan, and not setting it up so that the plan will be rubbished if schemes are included which are unlikely to materialise. Further, the plan lacks authority if it does not address the identified and agreed reasons for concern, or include a clear and achievable action plan with time scales, who will do what and reviewing processes.

Family situations where the FGC appeared to have worked well included where the carer – a single parent, or a weary grandparent – needed family support. Situations where contact arrangements needed negotiating also worked well. Some families were able to use the conference to re-open family communications which had broken down. And, finally, where relationships with previous social workers were negative, the provision of a neutral arena was clearly facilitating for some families, empowering them to make their own decisions.

Situations which are not suitable for FGCs included at times of crisis, such as where a child protection conference was in the offing, or where urgent requests for family placement were being made. There were some situations where the problems are unlikely to be stemmed by one FGC, such as in cases where the family is struggling to contain a difficult adolescent already accommodated. And, in this project, a few smaller families would have preferred a meeting in their own home.

Discussion

Early research from New Zealand and Australia suggested overall positive outcomes of FGCs, with families tending to reach more creative solutions to their difficulties than those proposed by professionals (Marsh and Crow 1998). They have subsequently been implemented in a number of countries including Canada, USA and several Scandinavian countries (Pennell and Burford 2000). In the UK, there is evidence that FGCs are now being more widely used than they were initially, and for a wider range of issues, including education (see Family Rights Group 2008).

However, despite the benefits for participatory practice and children's involvement, there are a number of complex issues around power sharing. One question raised by our as well as other studies is how families are defined. Who is invited and included are decisions which can be beyond the control of the family and, in particular, of the more vulnerable members, such as the child. And moving on to issues about process and management, there is also evidence here, as in Holland's (2006) study in Wales, that professionals continue to exert some control by, for example, taking responsibility for drawing up the plan.

Family dynamics can also control what is said and what decisions are made. Research in Canada suggested that FGCs were not effective with the most turbulent family relationships (Pennell and Burford 2000). Our study also raised concerns about how the interests and self esteem of the most vulnerable family members can be maintained, and that the voice of the child may be silenced by more powerful family members (see also Lupton and Nixon 1999). Dalrymple (2002) suggests that the family nexus in such meetings can be as institutionally excluding as in any other adult forum, and also potentially damaging. A key question is therefore whether there is a conflict between empowering the children and empowering the family group as a whole. And if there is, how can this best be managed to ensure the child's voice is heard and the experience is positive?

Lupton and Stevens (1997) and Crow and Marsh (2000) suggest that children participate more in FGCs than in other decision-making arenas, such as child protection conferences. In our study FGCs were in the main welcomed and valued by family members, children and young people and professionals alike. Even when the outcomes over the medium term were unclear, the engagement of children with their families as part of an ongoing process of working together and working with social services in a more equal enterprise seemed valuable as a means of securing better outcomes for the children.

On the evidence of the children involved here, FGCs provided a valuable and valued resource. They described experiences which were enjoyable in their own right, and valued the opportunity for resolving family conflicts and developing relationships. Based on the experiences of these children, and of the other studies cited, children's inclusion in FGCs is generally to be encouraged. Their responses suggested overall that they had valued the experience of being consulted, of being listened to and, on the whole, they had welcomed the opportunities for families to work together on issues free from the attentions of social services. When FGCs work well, the process could be described as part of a symbolic and cathartic healing process, and as enabling children to be involved in important family decisions that affect them closely.

Our findings concerning the children's understanding of the purpose and the process of the conferences also confirm other studies in demonstrating that children feel empowered by being consulted and are able to understand information given to them about issues which affect them. They highlight the importance of taking seriously children's views about whether they want to be present, who should be invited and what it is helpful to discuss in the meeting. FGCs thus have the potential to democratise family decision making by reducing power differences between professionals and families, and, in some cases, by reducing power difference within families.

A further key question concerns whether or not the children's presence in the conferences leads to improved outcomes for them and their families. The immediate outcome for most of these conferences was positive, for example extended families offering short-term care and helping with practical arrangements, and reported improvements in the children's behaviour – such as better school attendance or agreeing to work on problems. Significantly, new contact arrangements with non-resident fathers were made in seven cases. Within the scope of this study it was not possible to determine the relationship between the attendance of the children *per se* and improved outcomes. However, the children's stories and the parents' and practitioners' comments suggested that it is reasonable to hypothesise that the children's presence was an important factor in achieving change, at least in the short term.

Nonetheless, our study suggests that although FGCs can usefully include children and have a clear role in children's welfare practice, they are not the panacea for all ills or necessarily the route to empowering practice for all children or all families. Where there are contra-indications to children's presence, such as damaging family dynamics, other means of ensuring that the child's views are included need to be found. Our research suggested that the situations where FGCs work particularly well include situations where family support may be mobilised to help with a single carer or grandparent, where family communication, including contact with the non-custodial parent has broken down, and where relationships with social service departments have become negative or entrenched.

Implications for practice
It is important to involve the children in the reasons for having the FGC, what it is hoped to achieve and who should be included
The preparation undertaken by social workers before the meeting is an important part of the process. Both carers and children need to be involved in the preparatory stages, asked whether or not they want this process of decision making and to be informed about what it involves. The children should be seen alone.

Negotiations over what information is shared, and where and when the FGC is held, are necessary and can signal to the children a sense of ownership. While all family members need to be offered choice over who should be invited and the aims of the meeting, difficulties arose where the views of children and carers differed. Since the aims of the children may differ from those of their carers, clarity and honesty about what can be achieved at the outset, and the reasons for the choice, are important.

The children were helped by being well prepared, sometimes with the help of an advocate or informal supporter, and having formal or informal support from an adult to speak in the meeting. Writing down their thoughts and feelings before a meeting was also helpful.

Children will need time to assimilate information and ask questions

As in child protection conferences and review meetings children may have little power in this situation. Their agenda may be different from other family members, and their capacity to communicate less sophisticated.

The social worker should brief the convener and consider talking to family members about the child's needs and feelings and how support can be provided for the child.

It is necessary to work with the children on alternative ways of participating if they do not want to be present. To exclude children would be contrary to the purpose, although if children do not wish to be present then this should clearly be facilitated and followed up afterwards. Other ways of feeding the child's views into the meeting could be used – by advocates, in writing or drawing or by a laptop computer or video.

Clear information about the role of advocates is necessary

Where advocates are used, preparatory work is important. While, in this study, the presence of advocates from the Children's Rights Service was valued by some, others were hazy about whether or not they had been there. For some children, who had declined the offer of an advocate or did not have one, the experience of the conference had been somewhat disempowering. So, as the provision of advocates develops, one way forward would be to offer advocacy as a norm.

Children will need help in understanding the difference between advocates and social workers, and time and opportunity to consider and voice what they want their advocates to say on their behalf.

However, not all children need or want advocates, and there was evidence in this study that being given a chance to speak in person was empowering for them and helpful for the adults to hear.

The roles of convener and social worker need to be clear

The role of the social worker and convener in enabling the family to negotiate agreement and to obtain the views of the child before and during the meeting is important, skilled and time consuming.

In these conferences, the social workers took a minor role in preparation for the conferences, the work being carried out by the project conveners. Some children experienced the conveners' distance from social services as a real benefit and social workers helpfully took a back seat. However, some children felt let down. Again, clear information about the social worker's presence and role in the meeting is essential so that children can understand what is happening. If they express the desire for their social worker to be present this should be negotiable.

Careful thought needs to be given beforehand to the management by professionals, including open negotiation and briefing

For the children this experience was, in some cases, new and extremely positive. In many cases the adults listened to what they had to say and acted upon it – for example in the cases where contact was set up. However, some children felt at best uncomfortable and at worst victimised.

This suggests that, for some families, the FGC is not the most appropriate intervention, and that careful thought needs to be given beforehand to the management by professionals of the meeting. When this is negotiated openly, there is more likelihood that the different patterns of professional involvement will be considered appropriate for different situations, or that the best decision is to provide an alternative intervention.

Family dynamics need to be assessed and managed

There is evidence that, even where families have deep-rooted and long-standing relationship difficulties, this method of working together can facilitate communication and enable the children to be involved in decision making.

While the presence of advocates may ensure the child's voice is heard, the advocacy role does not include the management of damaging family dynamics. The social worker should give the convener a careful assessment of family dynamics beforehand to enable these to be handled in the meeting.

There are some family groupings where discussion of some issues is either unhelpful or disturbing – especially to vulnerable children. In these cases the social workers and/or the convener need to exercise control over who is present, what is discussed and how. There may also be issues of confidentiality and disclosures that require careful pre-planning by organisers, and the concept of private time needs careful thought and management as it is not always experienced as helpful.

The plan needs to be clear, achievable and agreed by all in the meeting

To achieve the carers' and children's co-operation and communicate respect, the plan should be agreed in the meeting, and the interests of the children clearly included in writing. Written plans should be made available for all family members. Where concrete arrangements are agreed these need to be followed up by the social worker, and the children kept informed of progress and supported.

CHAPTER 7

The Participation of Children in Initial Child Protection Investigations

'I was offered a chance to talk but they just kept asking the same questions over and over again – how are you? Have you got any problems? What would be helpful would be for us to 'ave a say and not just them.' (12-year-old boy, registered sexual abuse)

This chapter reports on the participation of 27 children in a child protection investigation and the subsequent reviews (Bell 2000b, 2002). The overall aim of the research study was to explore with the children their experiences of the child protection process, the degree to which they felt they had participated and the processes that hindered or facilitated this. More detailed aims were to obtain their views on participation in meetings, whether they had been offered choice or consulted about what services they wanted and how they were delivered and what they found helpful or otherwise from the range of professionals involved.

Child protection investigations take place where it is considered a child may have been, or is at risk of, suffering significant harm. The local authority is required by Section 47 of the Children Act (1989) to make enquiries to enable it to decide whether it should take any action to safeguard and promote the welfare of the child. Where there is risk of immediate harm emergency action may be necessary to secure the safety of the child. Some children are removed from home, as are some abusers. In some cases criminal proceedings will be put in train and run alongside the investigation and emergency removal to care.

Working Together (DCSF 2010) reiterates and confirms the earlier guidance under which investigations should proceed. First, information should be collected and analysed. A strategy discussion should then be convened, bringing together the range of professionals from health, education, police and other agencies who may be involved and the family. Following joint enquiries and the completion of a core assessment, in cases where the original concerns are substantiated a conference is held after 35 days. The purpose of the conference is to determine whether or not abuse has taken place, what it comprised and, if so, to set up a child protection plan. The plan now replaces registration on the child protection register, and should identify the risk factors, establish short- and long-term aims and objectives and identify the professionals that are responsible for different aspects of the work within specified time scales.

Ten days after the conference the core group of professionals, with the social worker as the lead, meets to develop the plan as a working tool. Three months later, and every six months thereafter, a review conference is held to consider whether the child protection plan should continue, be changed or discontinued. Under Section 12 of the Children Act (2004) each local authority was required to establish a social care IT system, accessible to all legitimate agencies, where essential information will be stored. All records of the investigation will be electronic, and stored on the Integrated Children's System (ICS).

Guidance and Local Safeguarding Board (previously Area Child Protection Committee) protocols stress the importance of listening to children's views and of involving them in all stages of the child protection investigation, from Section 47 enquiries through to the initial child protection conference, the following core group and reviews. The DfES (2005b) stresses that children must always be interviewed alone and separately. At each stage it is stressed that the views of children should be sought and expressed, that the record, minutes of meetings and the plans should be shown, discussed and negotiated with children and their agreement given to the interventions suggested.

> Before a conference is held the purpose of a conference, who will attend and the way in which it will operate should always be explained to a child of sufficient age and understanding... The child, subject to consideration about age and understanding, should be invited to attend and to bring an advocate, friend or supporter if s/he wishes. Where the child's attendance is neither desired by him/her nor appropriate, the LA children's social care professional who is working most closely

with the child should ascertain what his/her wishes and feelings are and make these known to the conference. (DCSF 2010, p.163)

So, while the guidance is clear that children's views should be sought and always made clear in the decision-making process, there is acknowledgement that not all children may be able to give a view, that the children's physical presence may not be appropriate and that a range of ways of expressing their views can and should be found.

Supporting the participation of children in all aspects of this serious and complex process, a process that is constructed for adults, obviously carries with it difficulties for all participants. As discussed in earlier chapters, from the perspective of the social workers heading up the enquiries, their capacity to place the children's participation at the core of their agenda is compromised by a range of difficulties. As agents of the authority, their first and primary duty is to protect the child from significant harm. They therefore need to balance the child's right to have a voice with the imperative to protect him. Clearly this locates the power in the hands of the social worker since it is the social worker who must, first, judge the child's capacity to understand and engage with the process. Such a judgement will be based on skill, knowledge and experience – but it is subjective. Age, for example, is not necessarily a determinant of capacity. Maturity is a relative concept. Young children may be unable to verbalise their views, in which case accessing them depends upon the skills and resources of the worker in using other materials, such as play, and in interpreting what they see accurately. Adolescent children may be traumatised and too confused or frightened to speak.

Particular difficulties arise when children have disabilities which impair their capacity to speak, or are learning disabled or do not speak English. Research has suggested particular difficulties for children from ethnic minority groups. Mars (1989) found that black female children were hampered from disclosing abuse for fear of a racist response, and Chong (2006) describes the language barriers in Chinese families. Where interpreters are required there may be insufficient time to establish the trust essential for the child to speak openly.

Second, in seeking the views of the child, social workers must balance the child's wishes against what they believe to be in the child's best interests. The two do not necessarily coincide. Here the conflict between enabling the child to be a child, and treating him as an adult is keenly felt.

A further conflict arises from the need to balance the rights of the adult – for example, for confidentiality and privacy, with the rights of the child – for example to full information. Some information, previously unknown to the child, may reasonably be considered to be damaging to the child in this context. For example, that his mother has had three children adopted, or that his father is a paedophile.

Third, while it is imperative and clear from the guidance that all children should be seen alone at all stages of the process, we know, following a number of serious case reviews (Brandon *et al.* 2008) and from public inquiries, that social workers can face a range of difficulties in seeing the child alone – especially in the short time scales between referral and conference. Some parents, like Victoria Climbié's aunt and Khyra Ishaq's mother, are intimidating and make such contacts extremely difficult. In some cases social workers reasonably fear violence. Edleson (1999) recorded a 30–60 per cent co-occurrence of domestic violence and physical abuse in his review of studies of child protection cases. In others the environment makes privacy difficult, or the child does not feel safe enough to be separated from his carers, or the carers forbid it.

Fourth, there is evidence that social workers have difficulty in engaging with traumatised children and defend against the pain of hearing their accounts of abuse. In Bell's (1999c) study of parents' involvement in child protection conferences, only 27 per cent of the social workers interviewed had seen the child before the conference, or talked to the child alone after it. Clearly good supervision is an important way of managing the anxiety generated. However, we know from SSI reports (Social Services Inspectorate 1997), and more recently from serious case reviews (Brandon *et al.* 2008) that it is not always available.

Turning to the perspectives of the children and the family, child protection investigations are frightening experiences. The children involved are often threatened by the involvement of strangers in their lives while at the same time they are experiencing their parents' lack of control over events. The investigation may happen suddenly and without warning, and the fears of family breakdown, of them thinking their parents are being punished or of their own removal from home are very real for the children involved. In some cases – for example where there has been a disclosure of sexual abuse or children think their behaviour has precipitated the professional involvement – the children feel guilty and responsible. Also in some cases the children will need to give witness statements to the courts. Conflicting loyalties arise and issues of power are fundamental and transparent.

The context of a child protection investigation is therefore central to children's capacity to participate in the process, from assessment through to conference and review. Participation depends upon a range of factors including children's ability to engage with and understand what is happening, to assimilate information, to form a view as to the outcomes they wish to achieve, to decide on how they wish to present their views and to trust the people involved. In considering whether and how their participation can be effected it is therefore important to know what experiences and feelings are provoked by the investigation – in carers, as well as in the children themselves. Gaining some understanding, also, of their views of the professionals who are carrying out the investigation is also key to considering how and who can facilitate their engagement in the process (see Bell 1996b, 1999c).

The study

The study which follows reports upon 27 children's experience of involvement in a child protection investigation. The findings give an account of the children's experiences and feelings when the investigation is launched, with some reference also to how these are mirrored by their parents. The account then follows the chronology of the enquiry, from assessment through to conference and review. The focus is on whether children felt able to or wanted to participate in the different aspects of the process, and on what facilitated this or got in the way.

Method

The cohort of children considered for inclusion in the research comprised all children aged between 8 and 16 who had been subject to a child protection conference in a small Northern city between 1998 and in 2000 and who were still in touch with social services two years later. From a cohort of 127 children, 27 were interviewed by the use of a semi-structured interview schedule, alongside some child-friendly visual aids and drawing materials. Twelve parents were also interviewed.

The sample

The 27 children were aged between 8 and 16, most (20) being between 10 and 16 years. Thirty-three per cent were looked-after children. The gender distribution was even. Four had learning disabilities, and one was non white British. The children came from 16 families: 11 from single parent households, five from reconstituted families, six lived with other relations and five of the looked-after children were in foster care. It is striking that the father was absent from 15 of the 16 households. In the one household containing a father, he was a single parent.

All categories of abuse were represented. The sample was thus diverse, containing boys and girls of all ages with differing care career paths and patterns of intervention, who were and were not on the child protection (CP) register for differing categories of abuse, from different class and ethnic backgrounds and including children with special needs. Looked-after children are proportionately over-represented, overall.

Findings

Children's understanding about the investigation

Many of the children were hazy regarding what the child protection investigation comprised. Fifteen believed they were on the child protection register, seven thought they were not and the remainder (five) did not know. Their understanding was not always correct. Many thought (correctly) that it had happened between two and three years ago. In some cases more then one investigation had taken place or the children had experienced social services involvement over a period of years. One 14-year-old girl, for example, had been in and out of foster care since the age of 4.

All but three of the cases were 'open', although many of the children themselves either did not understand this concept, or did not know if the case was open or not. Where cases were closed and contact had ceased children did not understand why. There was confusion where the parent was being visited, but the child was not. In some cases their carers were also confused.

A sense of bewilderment and fear at the start of the investigation is strongly communicated, as is the children's concerns about the impact on their mothers. The children's main recall of why the investigation was taking place was of the knock on the door which was scary. Their responses, overall, were determined by how safe they felt in their home and, in this respect, they comprise three groupings: those with mixed feelings, those that felt intruded upon and those who welcomed the safety offered.

MIXED FEELINGS

Most of the children had mixed feelings. They were initially worried and remained bewildered about what was happening. However, they also had some positive feelings in that they felt that they and their families were being helped. From a 14-year-old boy:

> 'Social workers got involved three years ago – to tell you the truth I felt nervous and cross…one thing, I didn't know why I needed a social worker in the first place. But now I know I needed help with my behaviour and stuff.'

UNWELCOME

The second group of children comprises those who lived in environments that were, at some level, warm and loving but where there were also worrying incidents. In these situations the children experienced the investigation as intrusive.

> 'I felt they poked their noses in. They were interfering with me and me mum's lives – I don't know how they got in. I felt upset – they took me off me mum.'

These children often needed to identify with or felt they should protect their mother. This aroused conflicting loyalties and deep ambivalence – especially, as will become apparent later, with regard to the relationships that they then allowed themselves to form with the professionals involved. From a 9-year-old girl:

> 'What was most helpful was when the social workers weren't around. I feel listened to and supported by my family.'

WELCOME

In this small group, the children were frightened either by their own or their carer's behaviour and, for them, the intervention offered welcome protection. From an 11-year-old girl:

mum hit me and I was confused and scared. I missed a lot of school. It felt strange at first. I wasn't really sure what would happen and I wanted to go into foster care. I feel much safer here. I am looked after and taken care of.'

First contacts

The environment in which first contact takes place is heavy with fear, suspicion and lack of trust. The largest group of children (11) said they felt worried, upset or scared when they were first visited. 'I was right nervous and started smoking' (14-year-old boy). Most expressed bewilderment about being caught up in something which was not in their experience and was beyond their control, and were apprehensive about what would happen. From a 14-year-old girl:

'The first time I saw a social worker it were strange, seeing someone just appear out of the blue. I had no idea what they could do. I hadn't heard about them before.'

Some feared being removed from home. This girl had an abiding memory of this fear. Three years after the investigation she was able to recall that she felt responsible for protecting her siblings. She was also able to list the professionals who visited the house:

'I'm worried about what social workers can do…the police came, then the social worker came, then the doctor came to examine G's bruises…I thought we might be taken away. I still worry about that.'

Anger and confusion, linked to a feeling of being out of control, was commonly expressed. In this case the 10-year-old boy recalls that some of the information he heard being discussed was incorrect:

'They were talking about stuff that I didn't know about and saying things that weren't correct.'

In contrast, two of the children described the removal from home as a relief – even taking into account changes of foster parents, characteristic of emergency removal from home. This 12-year-old boy said:

'The social worker took me to a new foster home because I'd run away. I was in there two days, then he took me to another one…that made things better.'

Many had vivid memories of their first contact with the professionals involved. All remembered being visited by social workers, most listing four or more by name. From an 11-year-old girl who had been physically abused:

'The first one seemed friendly, then I got one, then another one.'

The children's bewilderment was echoed by many of the parents. The quote below characterises the reaction of the parents in this study, drawing attention to the fact that their preoccupation with their own emotions will have the effect that there may be little energy available to support their children or listen to their views.

'When they heard my child had an injury, it was madness with the police and social workers turning up and all the neighbours watching, it was so embarrassing. I felt all that was unnecessary…there were lots of meetings then it all fizzled out…'

Understanding about why the investigation took place

Many of the children did not understand either the concept or the process of the investigation. Although half reported that their social worker had explained this process to them, this had either meant nothing to them, or they could not remember what had been said. Where they could recall what had been said, this was that a meeting would take place where the problems would be discussed. Most thought they would be moved, possibly into a foster home, or that they might be taken into care. A few (five) knew it was about putting them on the register, but most had no knowledge about the child protection register or what an ICPC could do.

Moving on to what information the children assimilated and remembered, most of them (19) said that the social worker had explained the reason for the visit. This 16-year-old girl said:

'They did explain to me why they were coming – it meant a great deal to me.'

Their understanding of the reasons for the visits was often in general terms such as sorting the family out, and keeping the family together.

'I was only 6. I was happy to see them. We needed help – we weren't getting on well in the family.'

A large number of the children believed the intervention was because of their bad behaviour: 'I was naughty'. Some thought that the reason for the investigation was to explore what help would be appropriate, such as counselling and help at school. Half understood the social worker's explanation, which generally tallied with what their parents told them. However, they felt angry and let down when the social worker did not communicate this directly with them. From a 14-year-old girl:

> 'The social worker didn't explain to me why she came. She explained to my mum and dad, but not to me. I felt quite annoyed 'cos it was something to do with me. I just thought they were friends of me mum and dad.'

This lack of direct contact deepened children's bewilderment and reinforced a lack of self esteem, resulting in them believing that they were not key parties and that their views did not matter. Directing the assessment mainly or purely at the adults gave an unfortunate message about whose views mattered. This 12-year-old girl said:

> 'I don't think I knew what he was here for 'til my mum said something about why he was here. He was normally always talking to my mum… so he didn't explain anything to me. No. I wasn't seen alone.'

The importance of gaining children's trust at this early stage in the investigation was clearly portrayed. First impressions are important in communicating to children that their views matter and that part of the professional's task is to prepare them for the ensuing conference process and to ensure that their voice is heard. In this study practice in this respect varied.

Meetings
THE ICPC
Of the six children in this study invited to attend the ICPC, only three chose to attend. Two found the experience daunting and would not go again:

> 'I had to go – but they didn't mean anything to me. There were other people involved…but I don't know who they all are. They just talk about everything – my life.'

And from a 14-year-old girl who had been sexually abused:

> 'They've had two. I went to the first one. It was so they could put me on the register – protects children from harm…I don't like it at all…being there…they talk about what's happened in the past and it brought it all back up – upset me and me mum and I don't like

seeing her upset. They wanted me there because they didn't like my mum's boyfriend – they wanted me to go against him – to speak out. I couldn't say much in front of those people – about me not liking him – but that's about all I could say. It wouldn't have made any difference if my mum wasn't there.'

These children describe a number of aspects of attendance which were difficult. First, the sense of exposure and feeling out of control was disempowering. Second, both of these children disliked others hearing the privacy of their family lives. They expressed concern at the numbers of professionals present – especially their teachers who 'stuck their noses in'. This concern is echoed by parents in Bell's (1999c) previous study who particularly objected to the inclusion of teachers who they saw every day and did not think should be allowed to hear intimate details about the family.

Ambivalence was also a feature. The third girl felt she had been put unfairly in a situation of conflict by being asked to publicly disclose information which could damage her mother. At the same time she said she felt supported. She feared being returned to a neglectful and violent home and found the experience positive and that she had been listened to. It is notable, however, that she was present for only part of the conference:

'I went to the first part of the conference – it was OK. They were finding things out and what I thought…they told me what had been decided – to sort out school, health and so on. I said I thought it would be best to go into care.'

Three who were invited chose not to go. Advocates were not available at this time, but they felt confident their social worker would represent their views. From a 16-year-old girl:

'I didn't want to go – nothing would have persuaded me. I didn't know what to say and got all confused. Me mum used to go and talk about school – and I just didn't want to hear about it – couldn't be doing with it. She asked me what I wanted to say so they could make my point in the meeting. She kept her word.'

In spite of their non-attendance, these three children said that they did receive information from their carer and social worker and did feel involved. This 13-year-old boy said:

'My mum told me about it. It was held to make us get on better as a family. The social worker came to tell me what had happened – and I do feel involved even though I wasn't there.'

Two children who had not been invited (for reasons not known to the researcher) wished that they had gone to hear what was said. They reported that they had been told what had happened by their mothers.

FURTHER MEETINGS

Because the focus of the ICPC is on considering risk and registration, the process laid down in *Working Together* (DCSF 2010) is for a core group meeting to be held ten days after the ICPC to consider and put in place a child protection plan. Commonly this is attended by professionals from the range of agencies that are carrying responsibility for the children who have been registered, and family are rarely included. Research evidence did suggest that, in fact, the interim time is generally regarded as breathing space, and little work is done (Calder and Horwarth 1999). At any rate, children are rarely included in this, or in the subsequent child protection meetings. Whether this has changed with the demise of registration in 2007 remains to be seen.

Reviews

More commonly, children who have been the subject of an ICPC and who are looked after are included in review meetings. The context and emotional climate of review meetings is different from ICPCs. In a number of cases, the children have been to one before – especially those who are looked after. Leaflets and materials exist to help them to prepare for what will be discussed, and, in many cases, the meeting reviews progress and is not decision making. Following the Green Paper, *Care Matters* (DfES 2006), independent reviewing officers now have the task of ensuring children are prepared beforehand. Most reviews are smaller and briefer than ICPCs, and the children are likely to know most of the participants.

However, as with the ICPCs, children's views on review meetings were mixed. Seven in this study had attended reviews. A common comment was that they were 'boring – for adults'. From a 14-year-old girl:

'I've been to some – they're just boring – they just talk about the same stuff over and over again...I don't feel it changes anything...I get me review notes back – about what everyone's been saying. They just tell you everything they've said, which I know already. I just put them away.'

However, some children, such as this 15-year-old boy, had valued review meetings which provided them with a forum for asking questions and clarifying what was happening:

'Later I went to a meeting with my mum because I'd got thrown out of school. I told people there that I wanted to live with my mum and I did think they listened to me and I listened to them.'

This 14-year-old boy also felt listened to and, as with the one quoted above, had a sense of influencing the decisions made:

'I went to the review meeting and actually asked some questions about home visits and where I should go and not go. I had some say in what was being decided…I asked him and my mum to have long weekends at home – and they arranged it. I felt really pleased to hear my mum say she wanted me home and I'm really glad that K and C supported me and decided I could go home.'

In most cases the children who had experience of reviews felt that they had been adequately represented whether they were present or not. There were particular problems for children with language and communication difficulties, suggesting that the use of signers or interpreters, as recommended in the recent guidance, is indicated.

Choice

One aspect of children's participation which is empowering to them is to be offered some real choices. We asked the children whether they had been offered a choice regarding the gender or race of the social worker, of being seen alone, of who they had to see and what was to be talked about. Where children have been sexually abused, the gender of the worker can be significant. Equally, the location and timing of the interviews will influence what is communicated.

Only two of the children in this study had been offered any choice regarding the gender or race of the social worker, where they saw them or when. For this 10-year-old boy his apparently healthy engagement with S is clearly facilitated by the fact that S is male and that he had a choice:

'I was asked if I wanted a lady or a man. We all wanted a man and got S. S said he was going to come and see us more often to see how we were getting on.'

The importance of seeing children alone has been discussed, and most of the children interviewed in this study had been seen alone at some time (i.e. with no family present). Those that had not resented it. Ten thought they could refuse to see one of the professionals, and four of them had. In the words of this 9-year-old girl:

'I was offered a choice who I saw and I talked about what I wanted to talk about, filling in those little booklets [consultations documents].'

This child's perception is interesting given the registration of sexual abuse. A number of cases being bought to conference involve medical and police investigations which can be physically and emotionally intrusive and threatening to children.

Turning to the children's input to the agenda of the review, a third thought the agenda was (sometimes) theirs. Nine did not, again echoing their experiences in child protection investigations where they had little or no control over events. In this case, the 15-year-old boy cites his experience in court:

'They rush their side of things when it comes to going to court…but they go slowly or not at all when it comes to my agenda.'

Again, a number of the younger children said that the social workers had talked to their mothers, rather than to them. They were pleased that their mothers were getting help, but also wanted attention in their own right. From a 12-year-old girl:

'I can remember the first social worker – it were J – he was an idiot. He was not helpful at all 'cos he talked to me mum all the time.'

Involvement, representation and influence

While a third of the children reported that they had been asked their views, the majority, like this 12-year-old girl, did not attach importance to this or see it as being part of a caring environment in which their views mattered:

'Influence? Nowt happens. They're just doing their job. I didn't know what had been decided. I didn't ask 'cos I didn't really understand. I don't think I influenced anything.'

There was a lack of clarity as to how representation might take place, although several had seen the reports and record written for the meeting.

In most cases the children knew what had been decided – sometimes their mother had told them. Most said that the decisions had made a difference to them, although only six believed they had influenced them. Some felt let down because what they said they wanted was different from what happened. This 14-year-old girl describes her experience of her wishes being ignored, signifying the difficulty of asking children for their views when it is not clear that their wishes can be met:

> 'Yes, they asked me if I wanted to go into care or back home. But then they didn't take any notice. I told them I wanted to stay in the children's home, and then they moved me…and then they moved me again. I'm sick of being moved.'

Similarly, this 16-year-old boy with learning difficulties thought the decision about his care had already been taken, and so asking for his views seemed tokenistic to him:

> 'I would have felt more involved if I had been invited to listen – but they told me about them after they'd happened. S wrote stuff down but I don't know what. It made no difference anyway, what I said, 'cos they decided dad should go to N.'

Clearly careful explanations need to be provided relating to what is possible, what cannot be guaranteed and what cannot be promised. In many cases the social worker will be uncertain, and is dependent on the shifting and scarce resources available in the authority. Munro (2001) suggests that the concentration in local authorities on quantitative performance indicators and the LAC forms (used to record details of looked-after children and the social work practice) used at the time may reduce the time available to spend with the child and impact adversely on practice. More recent research, to be described in more detail in Chapter 8 has evidenced that this is the case – that social workers using the ICS have less time to spend in direct work with the children (Bell *et al.* 2008; White; Hall and Peckover 2008).

Outcomes

Nearly all the children said they had been offered help, and most were positive about the help they had received. What had been experienced as helpful was having somebody they could trust, who was reliable and who they could talk to about what mattered to them – who listened and was supportive, that is, 'on their side', and took them seriously. Being questioned and going over old ground was said to be intrusive, pushy, interfering – not helpful, as illustrated by the quote from the 12-year-old boy at the beginning of this chapter.

Replies as to what they thought the social worker was trying to achieve varied, from 'sorting out the problems', to 'changing my behaviour', 'protecting me', 'getting me back to school'. Trips, camp, play schemes, etc. were generally valued – especially by younger children. Being helped 'to sort things out' figured – for example, arranging contact with siblings, promoting friendships, advising about careers. Moving house and moving school was experienced as positive by a number of children. And material help was valued, especially by children who clearly were from impoverished homes and were extremely relieved at being rescued from an intolerable home situation. However, while most children enjoyed such diversions – for some they were a real treat – they were of significance within a meaningful relationship rather than as a substitute for one: 'camp and clubs – good in a fun way, but not in other ways – don't really change anything.'

Did things improve?

Fifteen children replied that things had improved for them mainly at home, but also at school and in their health. In most cases, the improvement had lasted, as described by this 9-year-old boy:

> 'Since the ICPC things have got better because I've been going out and coming in at proper times and going to bed when I'm told. I'm fine now – my confidence has improved…speak better, sleep better… at school things are better because I used to fight nearly every day – but at this school I'm good.'

Some of the older children, like this 15-year-old boy, commented that they had learned to become more thoughtful and reflective:

> 'I try to think about things before I do it. Social workers have made things better for me by sorting things out.'

The best things were a named person to rely on, getting things sorted, moving house, not being in trouble. The worst were being forgotten, being pushed around, being discussed. Some children continued to find their home life difficult, and others expressed specific fears about possible consequences of the intervention which they feared would rebound on them. Echoing the problems raised earlier where children felt out of control of events, another 15-year-old boy thought that if he insisted on seeing his father he would be punished:

> 'I refused to see [the social worker] for a while and this made things worse. I didn't see the point of talking to her because it was about my feelings – only talking – that was it – and I didn't want her to see my dad. I knew he'd go mental – but she told him anyway. It was twice as bad 'cos my dad started marching me to school.'

The professionals they remembered

SOCIAL WORKERS

Since most Children's Departments organise their work around duty, assessment and long-term teams, it is extremely likely that more than one social worker will be involved in the initial investigation. All the children remember being visited by social workers – many list four or more by name. It is therefore striking that in nearly every case one social worker is identified as being helpful, and has been a significant person in that child's life.

> 'I've had loads of social workers. S was a nice person – a nice lass – with the right manner to go about it…'

The children can clearly describe the professional and personal attributes they associate with helpfulness and unhelpfulness. Professional attributes include being reliable and sharing written records. Personal qualities are based on attitude – treating children with respect, 'being nice, friendly…taking us seriously'. This 16-year-old girl is able to describe what, in addition to the social worker's manner, was helpful:

> '…we wouldn't just talk about my family – she would ask stuff like did Bloggs touch you and then she'd ask how I was – she was concerned about me – it was like I could talk to her about problems if I had them – like a best mate.'

This quote also demonstrates the importance to the child of the quality of the relationship between child and social worker, and suggest some factors that contribute to it. The value of being listened to was mentioned by all the children – well illustrated by this 14-year-old girl:

> 'She listened and took me seriously and supported me. This stopped me being bad. E was a nice woman – she listened and cared.'

The need for social workers to be emotionally as well as physically available was also communicated by the adult carers – in this case the foster carer of an 8-year-old boy with learning disabilities:

> 'The best thing has been being able to talk to them at any time – N and L rang me twice daily and visited twice weekly – it was brilliant… there's always someone there for us and for A.'

Other professionals

EDUCATION

After home, school is the place which is most significant in the children's lives. Approximately one third of the children mention teachers who were either involved in the investigation, or who were subsequently helpful/unhelpful in school afterwards. Teachers who are helpful are genuinely concerned, available, provide concrete help, such as addressing bullying or providing extra teaching; those that aren't 'shout', 'don't listen', 'don't take us seriously'.

HEALTH

Few children recalled seeing health professionals. Some mentioned GPs, school nurses and an adolescent psychiatric unit. Experiences were mixed. Otherwise health professionals were seen as part of life and not exceptional – except in cases (probably sexual abuse) where their intervention was resented.

POLICE

Six of the children mentioned contact with police. Where they elaborated, they had been 'scared', and were seen as being more to do with the abuser than with being abused.

OTHERS

Regarding other professionals, nearly half of the children did not know whether others were involved who they had not seen; the remainder believed no one else was involved. What is highlighted here is the importance of the quality of relationship with an adult in the child's professional network.

Discussion and implications for practice

This study replicates findings from others on the involvement and participation of children and young people in meetings and reviews (see also Katz 1995; Scutt 1998; Dalrymple 2002; Sanders and Mace 2006). Generally, they are constituted for adults and are experienced by children as intimidating. Whether, as Scutt suggests, they can be made more informal seems unlikely because of the tension and anxiety present in all parties because of the nature of the enquiry. Vis and Thomas (2009) found that children needed to attend more than one meeting to participate effectively, and noting small gains was helpful. It is also possible that the key purpose of the ICPC, to make judgements about abuse and care, could be compromised by children's presence. Professionals in Bell's earlier study (1999c), and in Shemmings' (2000) study said their open reporting could be compromised through fear of upsetting children.

One of the most effective ways of promoting children's participation is through a relationship of trust by active listening, acceptance and reliability

A common finding across research studies is that children feel safer and can engage more effectively if they trust their social worker. In some cases their preferred confidante may be their teacher or another professional in their network. This needs to be acknowledged and supported by all participants.

Believing the child, taking what they say seriously and guiding without taking control underpin positive social worker–child relationships. Continuity of workers is essential. As in Munro's (2001) and McLeod's (2010) studies of looked-after children, all children mentioned the importance of one social worker in their lives, and were able to describe their qualities of trust, reliability, listening, acceptance.

Children need careful preparation for all of the meetings

Children are frightened, confused and can be angry about the investigation, so careful preparation for the ICPC and reviews is important. Time must be spent with the child before and after the meetings to ensure they know what will and has happened, and are provided with ongoing support. All children should be seen alone. Where possible, choices should be offered about the gender and race of the social worker and the location and timing of contact. Where interpreters or advocates are needed they should meet the child before the meeting and be briefed about the process.

A range of methods of engagement need to be available, taking into account the child's age and ability. With younger children toys and play will be useful. With older children exercises, books and computers could be used. All children with disabilities should have a social worker who is trained in appropriate communication techniques and has worked with them before the meeting to determine what they want to say and how.

Confidentiality and respect for the child's views have to be carefully balanced with safeguarding issues

Concern about the numbers of professionals in ICPCs and reviews is a common finding, and the chairperson needs to carefully consider which professionals really need to be there and for what purpose.

A sense of intrusion and concerns about confidentiality led to children's reluctance to share their views. Wherever possible, children's permission needs to be sought for confidential information to be shared and, in some cases, a balance has to be struck taking into account the cost of losing children's willingness to confide.

Practitioners may have the best of intentions in protecting children from risky situations, but the skill is to balance and continually renegotiate this with children so that they can appreciate the risks and comprehend the issues.

The size and formality of meetings needs to be carefully addressed

Children's experiences of the management of meetings is mixed. While most wanted to know what was being said about them and needed assurance that their views were being represented, they were frightened by the size, formality and adult language and structure of both reviews and conferences, and lacked conviction that they would influence the decisions made.

The role of the chairperson is key to ensuring children feel included, that the language used is user friendly and jargon free, and ensuring their views are heard. Independent reviewing officers should always see the child alone before the meetings and, where necessary, involve interpreters or advocates at an early stage.

Issues of concern to the child need to be identified and addressed

Children expressed concern that they were unable to become involved in decisions about the issues that really mattered to them, such as contact with their birth family. For older children who wanted more autonomy and influence, this was problematic, reinforcing, as it did, their lack of mastery and low self esteem. Their social worker should ensure their issues are presented to the meeting, even if they are unattainable.

Practitioners need to manage risk, while at the same time ensuring children know and hear that their views are being represented, and feel they are taken seriously. Clarity and honesty about what is achievable is necessary.

Children need to be involved in the records used in the meetings

Children's engagement in the process can be enhanced from the outset by their views being clearly recorded and their records signed by them. Where the records are electronic, laptops will be needed.

A further difficulty arising from electronic records is that a hard copy of each report for each child in the family to be conferenced needs to be produced for all participants in the meeting. The amount of paper is unwieldy and cumbersome – especially where there are a number of children in one family. Social workers should ensure that the views of each child are accurately included in the documentation, and that each child has read what it is appropriate for the child to know in the conference reports.

The most appropriate method of representation needs to be discussed with the child

Participation is not synonymous with attendance; a broader approach to ways of engaging children in child protection work, providing them with complex information about process and acquiring and feeding their views into the meeting is indicated. Some authorities have leaflets available for this purpose.

Children's preferred means of representation need to be discussed with them before the meeting. Social workers need to exercise judgement, and if necessary take control over the final decision. Where children wish to be present and their social worker thinks this appropriate, all participants need to be informed about their presence before the meeting. The chairperson needs to manage the meeting so that the experience is positive and the child feels included. The agenda could specify a point at which the child's views are presented.

The chairperson needs to manage potential conflicts of role in the meeting

Some children choose to have an advocate rather than to be present themselves, so local authorities need to support the provision of independent advocacy services. Some authorities, such as Wiltshire (Webb 2006) do report increased participation by young people aged over ten through advocacy, both in terms of their attendance and as reflected in the child protection plan. However, the role of advocates is not straightforward nor necessarily provides a solution to the problems identified here.

While they can play an important role in ensuring children's voices are heard, their role is additional to, not a substitute for, that of the social worker. Potential role conflict needs careful handling by the chairperson before and during the meeting, and the child needs help to appreciate their differing roles.

Not all local authorities have an advocacy facility. Where advocates are unavailable and children are not present, their views should always be presented to the meeting by the social worker and other professionals who know them and they should put these in writing or symbolic form to be tabled.

Support following the ICPC and reviews is essential

Children should be seen as soon as possible after the meeting and told what has been decided. Intensive ongoing support may be necessary, especially if the children are removed from their parents and legal actions are in train.

CHAPTER 8

The Participation of Children in Social Work Electronic Records

Boy: 'They've asked me about my family and my views on like family life and situations that happen, but that's it.'

Researcher: 'OK. How did you feel about being asked about things like that?'

Boy: 'I don't mind but some things I don't like talking about.'

Researcher: 'Why is that? Because you think its too personal or...?'

Boy: 'Yes.'

Researcher: 'It feels a bit intrusive?'

Boy: 'Yes.' (12-year-old boy)

'It's an ongoing problem that we, in the very nature of our work, need more time to be able to record meaningfully children's information and allow them time to communicate their needs and I guess the knock-on is that we feel that because there's so much more input on the keyboard and needing to be in the office to do that, you've actually got less time to do that.' (Social worker)

The focus of this chapter is on the involvement of children and young people by their social workers in the electronic records that are now kept of their assessments and plans. It reports on an evaluation undertaken between 2004 and 2006 on service users' views of the Integrated Children's System (Bell *et al.* 2007, 2008). The research findings and discussion pick up on a number of issues raised in the previous chapters, demonstrating the pivotal role recording processes have in involving the young people in decisions about their care. And it takes forward existing studies of children's involvement in recording (Cleaver and Walker with Meadows 2004) and adds to it by its focus on their involvement in the new electronic recording system, the Integrated Children's System (ICS).

As public inquiries have demonstrated time and again – most recently that following the death of Peter Connelly – the keeping of good, up-to-date records about the children's lives and the ongoing log of professional contacts with them and their families is of fundamental importance to their safety and wellbeing. Good practice requires that the recorded assessments of need are detailed, based on an analysis of children's development and family dynamics, and that the ongoing interventions and plans are appropriate. It is also essential that the chronology of the ongoing work enables close monitoring and supervision of each social worker's contacts with the children in her care.

Good practice also dictates that all the service users involved, including the children, have contributed to their assessments and plans and that the records evidence their involvement in and agreement to what is written down. Not only is this ethical. As previously argued, their direct involvement in recording promotes participatory practice and further means that they are more likely to work toward change where they have agreed with the assessments that are made of their problems and their needs and the consequent plans for change. In this respect the participation of children and young people in the writing of their social work records has the same outcomes as those described in previous chapters. That is, their direct involvement in the work means that their views are taken seriously, it communicates respect which promotes their self esteem and, at the same time, is more likely to ensure their participation in the work – and therefore lead to better outcomes.

The importance of involving young people in their social work records has long been recognised. As was clear from the previous chapter reporting on young people's participation in child protection conferences and reviews, young people have a key role in contributing to the sharing of information and checking that the information recorded is accurate and up to date. They are also more likely to work in partnership with practitioners if they have been party to the strategic planning. However, research on recording prior to the ICS has suggested that, despite government guidance on good practice, it was rare for social workers to provide children with copies of their assessments; neither were they expected to record that they had informed them about them. The children's views were not generally sought for child protection conferences, and for care plans, the social workers did not routinely tell the children what they were (Cleaver *et al.* 2004).

Prior to the Assessment Framework in 2000, there was no nationally agreed format for the records held by social services departments, and all records and reports were kept in hard copy on files. In 2004, the Children Act required all children's services authorities in England and Wales to establish and operate electronic information-sharing databases, and social work records had to be computerised and standardised nationally. Twenty-six electronic records were constructed, based on the forms and scales of the Assessment Framework, and involving a single approach to the key processes of assessment through to review based on children's developmental needs, parenting capacity and ecological factors. All social work records are thus now held on an electronic database. At the time this study was conducted they comprised the series of 26 standardised forms described above, although, as from 2010, children's departments can now create more flexible forms to meet local needs.

The esocial care record is called the Integrated Children's System which was introduced in 2004, and is used for four main groups of children: children in need, including those in need of protection and living at home; looked-after children; permanency options including adoption; and care leavers. The supporting guidance, *Working Together* (DCSF 2010) contains the requirement that children's views are recorded at each stage of the process. And the ICS is intended to be understandable to the children and families and informed by them.

The benefits and drawbacks of electronic recording by social workers

The move from paper to electronic recording is timely and, in the long run, necessary and desirable. There are a number of potential benefits in using computers as one of a variety of means of enabling young people to participate in some of the processes from assessment to review. There are also some limitations.

The benefits

As reported earlier, many children are comfortable using computers. The Good Childhood Inquiry (Children's Society 2009) found that a third of the 1800 children interviewed said they could not live without a computer, while 64 per cent of those aged 8–15 had access to the internet at home. Children and young people are generally more confident in using computers than adults. And technology clearly has the potential for facilitating their participation, particularly in the arena of policy making. For example, in evaluating a project in Scotland to incorporate young people's views into policy making, Borland *et al.* (2001) acknowledged that on-line consultation did offer important opportunities to participate. As previously described, this is of particular importance for national and international communications.

It can also be argued that, for some children, on-line communication is more productive than face to face. It is possible that computers could enhance self disclosure and promote more open sharing of sensitive information precisely because they do not involve face-to-face contact. They could also enable young people and children with communication difficulties to control the pace of the interview and allow them to progress the dialogue from the general to the personal in their own time.

Computers can also be used for one-to-one work. Davies and Morgan (2005) demonstrate how asking questions electronically in a graphic and stimulating computer-based context can be an important means of getting children's views. They developed a computer-assisted self-interviewing application, Viewpoint Interactive, which allowed young people to answer questions privately, in their own way and in their own time. Approximately one third of local authorities in England and Wales are now using Viewpoint Interactive to prompt young people to think about their care, and to consult them in advance of their reviews. Some have extended its use to the core assessment process and reviews. In My Shoes (see Calam *et al.* 2005) is another computer-assisted interview for communicating with children, to help them talk about difficult or troubling experiences.

Tregeagle (2006) suggests another benefit of the use of computers: that since the level of grammar and spelling required for internet communication is less stringent than written text on paper, young people may feel in more control of language. However, his suggestion that it could avoid potential literacy problems is not supported by more recent research (Kakabadse *et al.* 2009) which concluded that modern technology was worsening spelling and concentration and disrupting lessons.

The drawbacks
A TOOL-CENTRED APPROACH TO COMMUNICATING WITH CHILDREN

A potential limitation of using computers to communicate with children in need is raised by Connolly (2005). He used a computer-based assessment tool with children referred to a child and family psychiatry clinic and found that the use of new technology had no effect on some aspects of the assessment process, in particular the amount of information collected from children. From the children it elicited fewer statements and was seen to allow less spontaneity and imagination in their responses. He concludes that the 'higher-level interaction' needed for communicating with children, and eliciting their response, cannot be left to new technology. In his view, computer communication cannot replace a face-to-face relationship.

Given the consistency of the findings from the previous research studies – that for many children their involvement in the social work process depends upon the establishment of a good relationship, and time to talk – Connolly's research highlights the importance of direct work. The ICS study reported here, and supported by White, Hall and Peckover (2009), found that one of the main complaints from social workers was the time spent sitting in front of the screen filling in the tick boxes and standard sections that the ICS forms require. This has been estimated at 80 per cent of their time: time they could otherwise have spent in direct contact with the children and young people they were working with. A further concern is that the number of designated sections and boxes to be completed means that the narrative of the story can get lost. So, as Munro (2005) argues, while technology has an important role to play in practice, it is a user-centred rather than a tool-centred approach to communicating with children that facilitates good practice.

MANAGING CONFIDENTIAL INFORMATION

Another limitation of the use of electronic recording is that the issues of power and professional judgement, discussed previously, remain. There will always be some cases and some parts of the social work record which will need to be kept confidential, and there may be some bits which it would be unhelpful, at that particular time, for the young person to see. Adoption records would be a case in point. This problem, again, brings into the frame the dependence on the judgement of the practitioner, as well as the nature of the case. While the same issue appertains to paper records, it is likely to be more difficult for some social workers – especially those not confident with technology – to manage sensitive, confidential material that is on the record on screen. This may result in the children not seeing their records at all.

Tregeagle and Darcy (2009) point out that some social workers may feel uncomfortable with the ICT competence of young people, which is better than their own. They may not feel suited to this way of working and may have concerns about on-line communication which remain unresolved. Although, it could be argued, these resistances may change over time, the research evidence is that practitioners are not doing joint work on recording on the Integrated Children's System.

SECURITY AND CONFIDENTIALITY

Issues of security and confidentiality are always raised, including by children, about who has access to their records, and where they are stored. Paper records can and have been lost, stolen or inadvertently seen by the wrong person. However, these problems are compounded by electronic records because of the potential for much wider access to them. There are a number of reasons why electronic databases can be insecure, such as access to passwords, stolen or hacked-into files, availability to other agencies, government, etc.

SURVEILLANCE

As well as security and confidentiality, concerns have also been raised, generally, about the potential for increased surveillance that the operation of databases makes possible (Garrett 2005). The linking of the ICS system with Contact Point and the Common Assessment Framework (CAF) heightened concerns about surveillance. Contact Point was a government database, set up in response to the Climbé Inquiry, to log data on all children in England. As a result of concerns about surveillance it was scrapped in 2010 by the incoming Coalition government. In so far as promoting children's empowerment is concerned, feeling spied upon implies a lack of trust and adult control – and so is disempowering. Prout (2000) has suggested that practices directed at greater surveillance reduce both the adult's confidence in children's autonomy, and children's sense of control over the system which is managing their lives. For children with disabilities, who are often subject to greater surveillance anyway (see Priestley 2000), this electronic process of surveillance could increase their sense of disempowerment.

The new social work recording systems being used are thus an important dimension of current practice which bring with them the potential benefits and drawbacks outlined above. Whether they further or promote children's participation in their records and in the process of making assessments and decisions about their future was one aspect of the Integrated Children's System that was explored by this research.

The study

The study of the ICS was undertaken in two authorities in England and two in Wales between 2004 and 2006 (Bell *et al.* 2007). The three aspects presented here are those which evaluated children's participation in the ICS, which comprised:

1. Interviews with the young people and their carers.

2. Questionnaires and focus groups conducted with social workers and managers.

3. The disability substudy, comprising interviews with the families of disabled young people, with the young people themselves and with their social workers.

The aims were to explore the experiences of the ICS of the young people, their carers and their social workers. The focus here is on the extent to which they and their practitioners felt the ICS enabled and encouraged the participation of the young people in their assessments, meetings and recording.

1. Young people and their carers

To evaluate young people's knowledge and experience of the ICS, ten young people were interviewed. Five were male and looked after; of the other five females two were children in need and three were on the child protection register. Only two had experienced a previous system of recording.

Seven of their carers were interviewed, three of whom were birth parents, three foster carers and one the key worker from a residential care home.

FINDINGS
THE YOUNG PEOPLE

None of the ten young people interviewed were aware that a new system of finding and storing information was being introduced in their children's department. Seven had no knowledge of ICS. One young person clearly knew about the ICS from his social worker, responding: 'He came round a little while ago and told us about it.' What is less clear was whether the worker was briefing the young person because he had agreed to be involved in this research. The young people were therefore unable to compare the ICS to previous systems.

A number of the young people talk about social workers using paper and making notes. Reviewing the implementation of the ICS across the four sites, none of them were issuing social workers with laptops, palmtops or the like to enable data collection in the field to be electronic. Certainly the young people, when they made an observation, referred to paper:

'They use paper a lot. Because my social worker used to sit there with a pen and folder, a big folder of paper.'

However, they were not ill-informed about electronic communication. All but one had access to a computer, and used computers themselves for chatting with friends, looking up information, and as part of school work. They were not worried about the development of computer records, as such. They *were* concerned about what happened to them, who had access and how securely they were stored.

When asked where they would prefer to have their records stored, views were mixed. One said he would prefer to have his stored on paper, four had no strong feelings and two were unsure. Positive views were founded on safety – that since a password would be required to view the information, it was more secure. They thought they were less liable to damage or loss than paper files, and that storing records electronically would bring benefits in terms of efficiency:

'…you can keep more database on it can't ya, you can keep, keep more files on it and that… And it's quicker and easier.'

However, while most had little interest in the way in which information about them was recorded, some were concerned about the confidentiality of the records and who was allowed access to them:

'I think they should make it [the way in which social services store records] more confidential because they seem to be showing it to like loads of people.'

The young people found it difficult to understand core aspects of the system. They said that the processes from assessment to review were taking longer to complete than before. When asked what they were told about their assessments and care plans – whatever system was being used – most said that when information was provided, it was generally useful and provided in good time. Others were less positive:

'…information's not there. There's not enough information for me to say oh right, yeah, I understand why they're doing this.'

Regarding experiences of assessments, views were split between those who found them understandable and felt as though they were listened to during the assessment meetings and those who had trouble understanding what was said, or found the experience overwhelming and 'scary'.

None of the young people we interviewed made a direct contribution to their ICS records. None recalled having written directly on any form of ICS record. Some recalled being offered the opportunity to look at the information that had been recorded about them, but they declined because they were not interested in seeing it:

'I had a chance to, but I didn't really want to, because what they've written about me, they've written about me, I don't really care what they wrote because it's only a few words, if it's nasty.'

Their experience was supported by the findings from a separate survey undertaken of a study of 152 ICS records. These showed that no service user's views were recorded directly. Where the views of young people were included it was those expressed by their social worker or, more commonly, the chairperson of their meetings.

REVIEWS AND PLANNING MEETINGS

Most of the young people who had attended reviews felt as though they were listened to and that the review was understandable to them. Some expressed considerable ambivalence and negativity. One chose not to attend. Another said that she typically arrives at the review, asks the social worker if there is anything new to talk about and then, once she is aware of any significant changes, leaves the reviewing officer and her social worker to complete the meeting. Another said she often became exasperated during reviews because she felt that once the people present had formed an opinion about a particular aspect of her life, there was no way she could persuade them otherwise:

'I end up gettin' dead angry and just going mad so I just don't go.'

For these young people, as with those in the initial child protection conferences, the most important thing was their relationship with their social worker, and what outcomes they could expect. They spoke most favourably of the interpersonal aspects of service provision, such as the amount of time spent with their social worker and the extent to which they felt they were being understood and listened to.

THEIR CARERS

The experiences of the carers reflect those of the young people. None had heard of ICS, or knew recording systems were changing. They only knew about it because of the research. One carer said the information she received now was better, but seemed unsure as to whether this was due to a change in the system of storing information or more to do with the personality of her social worker:

'I would like to think it's to do with a change in the system, that's what I would like to think it's to do with, more than just it depends on what social worker you get.'

Like the parents in the disability study to be described later, one foster carer expressed concern that the language on the forms was hard to understand:

'...it's like the wording, the words are so like long, instead of being like OK to use the words that people know what they mean because you know some people you think "what does that mean?"...I mean

OK they've got more education and everything, but I'm just a normal person and I don't know half of these big words.'

Generally, carers' experiences of assessments were positive. Typifying their views of the social work process generally, experienced foster carers who had developed a close personal relationship with social workers were the most positive. There were, however, some negative comments. One carer said her assessment was unpleasant. She said she had felt intimidated during the assessment, and that she was not provided with adequate information in advance. Again, her experience reflected her relationship with her social worker – in this case, a negative one:

'I didn't like it. So I nearly lost my temper, but then realised that if I did lose my temper I would then give them exactly what they wanted. So I just sat there and cried basically, I cried at the end of the table because it was foul, it was horrible. But once we got the next social worker she was brilliant. It was like a completely different experience.'

Like the young people, no carers remembered making any direct contributions to ICS records. All said that they were afforded the opportunity to look at the records that were being made but had not contributed to them. Some of the carers, especially experienced foster carers, linked their relationship with their social worker with appropriate service delivery. This was important to them and seen as being more important than the systems in which social workers stored information. As this carer said:

'Paperwork's all very well but it loses a lot as well doesn't it…whereas if you're face to face and got relationships with people, you know, then you're going to share a lot more.'

In relation to reviews, like the young people, the carers' experience was that ICS reviews seemed longer and more detailed:

'With it being, you know, the one with new paperwork and all these… the way it's done it's quite different to normal and it took a lot longer than our normal review, if you see, what I mean?… It just, you know, seemed very long-winded compared to normal.'

2. The social workers

THE SAMPLE

To capture the social workers' experience and usage of the ICS, we ran ten focus groups at the beginning of the study and two at the end in three local authorities in England and Wales. At the end of the study 52 social workers from three local authorities, comprising 35 qualified social workers, five senior social workers and 12 unqualified workers completed questionnaires.

The presentation below focuses on the social workers' perception of the impact of the ICS on their capacity to involve children in recording and in the decision-making process.

FINDINGS

Overall, some positive comments were made about the ICS. It was supported in principle and the view was widely expressed that ICS had, potentially, a lot to offer. 'The principle of it is very helpful' was a typical comment. Satisfaction with ICS tended to be higher (but not significantly higher) among those who were more used to computers, though social workers who had used computers at work previously were less satisfied with ICS than those who had not had this experience.

However, experiences of using the ICS were predominantly negative. The respondents felt it was overly prescriptive and repetitive. Eighty-three per cent said it was time consuming – thus removing social workers from their core tasks of seeing clients. Initial and core assessments took up slightly more time than direct contact with the family or child. Only 11 per cent thought it user friendly and they were concerned that it lost the overall picture and did not provide user-friendly outputs for children and parents:

> 'I've been a social worker for a long time…ICS is excessively time consuming and over complicates information gathering. It is not user friendly for social workers and completely useless for clients… I find I can spend an inordinate amount of time sitting in front of the screen… Time I could spend with clients.'

The time required for recording was considerable. Completed initial assessments took a mean time of 10.19 hours, completed core assessments took 48.14 hours, completed child care plans took 27.4 hours and completed reviews took 36.81 hours. A small group of cases (e.g. young children at risk) made extreme demands on time, thus affecting the average.

Another criticism was that the forms were too lengthy for children and parents to cope with:

'I mean, you're talking about a 25-page document for a review of a service, with client/family groups that are in many cases in impoverished circumstances and to be presented with a document of that type is simply overwhelming... And for myself I find it quite overwhelming. And that's on a professional level. And I know which bits to skip...I know where to look. I'm not a client or service user literally...having to go through every section in order to try and find out what I want to. I think they are very, very un-user friendly.'

The language used in the forms was also criticised as being difficult for both practitioners and children to understand, and the volume and density of information required from the exemplars was seen as intrusive:

'I think we have to be careful really not to dehumanise in the process, 'cos this is people that we are working with, and when you get into using language like that and, you know, 20-page long documents for a review of services you've been providing, you kind of risk, I think, alienating people and leaving people feeling like they have been picked to pieces.'

The general reaction to the forms varied from the bemused to the negative:

'I bring them out and they can sit there and they roll their eyes, as soon as they see the size of that paper, they glaze over.'

A further concern raised by participants in the focus groups was that the ICS system led to a practical conception of social work as resting less on individual skill and more on observance of procedures. This concern lay behind the discussion of the impact of the system on work with families, the complaints about the time spent in front of a computer and the dislike of a method of analysis that was perceived as form driven, mechanical and ill adapted to individual clients. In essence this was that the system challenged the role and values of social work. One social worker put the point clearly:

'It's not us getting used to a radical new system. I think it's over and above that. It's challenging our role and asking us to redefine our role essentially to become, ultimately, at the end of the day, it only really matters if we fill the boxes in.'

A big question, therefore, is whether the ICS can enhance the interpersonal relationship which is the backbone of enabling children to participate safely. In itself, there is no reason why well-designed electronic records could not save the time practitioners spend recording, and there is potential for imaginative electronic tools to be created and used in their work. However, the design, length and complexity of the ICS at this time did not encourage or facilitate at all the involvement of young people in recording or in discussing plans – and therefore, in their participation in the social work process. Most importantly, practitioners did not like it, did not find it user friendly, and it did not result in nor push them toward participatory practice. As noted in Cleaver *et al.*'s study, 'the formality and length of the exemplars negatively impacted on their ability to work with families' (2008, p.188).

3. The disability substudy

In order to evaluate the use of ICS with different groups of children and young people Mitchell and Sloper (2009) conducted a separate substudy of disabled children, their families and their social workers. The particular focus reported here is on the capacity of the ICS records to facilitate the participation of these children and their parents or carers in their assessment and care plans.

SAMPLE

Twenty-two families at different stages of the assessment/review process were interviewed. This included seven children aged over 12, with a range of disabilities including Down's syndrome, cerebral palsy, learning disabilities and autistic spectrum disorders. The children were interviewed using a tool kit of rebus symbol-based flashcards. Rebus symbols are symbols or pictures that represent a word or syllables. For example, two gates and a head means Gateshead. They were asked about their participation in the social work process, from assessment through to review. The 16 social workers who had conducted each family's assessment/review were also interviewed.

FINDINGS
THE YOUNG PEOPLE

All the seven children interviewed had been in receipt of social work services for some years, and spoke positively about it. Because of their disabilities they were dependent on their social workers for access to their records, be they paper or ICS records. They did not know about ICS. The social workers said they had not explained ICS to these children because they found a number of aspects of the records inappropriate, not suited to all families and frequently meaningless for the children. Communication was difficult because the records were based on the written word, in language that was sometimes inaccessible or jargonistic. To communicate effectively, symbols needed to be used.

Assessments: None of the children had been actively involved in initial and core assessment meetings between their parent and social worker, or in reviews. They said they were happy for their mum or the social worker to speak for them. They recalled having been asked questions although they could not remember specifics, such as 'what things they would like more or less help with'. As far as the children were concerned, effective communication was based upon their relationship with their social worker and the dialogue, not upon the recording forms. It was the relationship with the social worker which had enabled them to take part.

Reviews: Some parents said they preferred their children to be present in reviews, both because it was better for the children and because the professionals needed to see their children's disability. Two would have welcomed the social worker's greater engagement with their children. Where children had not attended, the parents felt that was appropriate because of their impairments, and thought it could be intimidating for them:

> 'I don't think it would mean an awful lot to him, not really, no. He knows we're there, he knows we're there for a meeting but how do you tell him? We could tell him there was a meeting with lots of people there but I don't really know that he'd fully comprehend, it's not something he's ever participated in…so, in Andrew's case, you know, if he was a perfect talker than yes, I would have said yes, it's very important that you've got the young person's viewpoint, what they want out of life and where they want to be and how they want to

achieve it, yes, but not in Andrew's case, 'cos he can't express himself well enough, that's my idea anyway, it wouldn't gain anything.'

Advocacy: The use of advocacy, particularly in formal meetings, has been discussed elsewhere in this book as a helpful way of involving children. Where children are, because of their disability, often dependent on their parents for expressing their views, advocacy could have a particularly important role to play in considering future needs. However, being offered the services of an advocate for their child was not important for most of these parents.

Their social workers

Over half of the 16 social workers in the disability substudy thought that the ICS would lead to reduced participation and involvement for disabled children. First, they felt that the time taken inputting data would reduce the time available to spend with the child:

'It's an ongoing problem that we, in the very nature of our work you need more time to be able to record meaningfully children's information and allow them time to communicate their needs and I guess the knock-on is that we feel that because there's so much more input on the keyboard and needing to be in the office to do that, you've actually got less time to do that.'

Second, direct work with the children was often slow because of communication disabilities, because the forms were only available in the written word and because the format and language used was seen as being inaccessible and unappealing to children. Children's views were often communicated in a visual format, such as photos and symbols. This meant that the social workers were more reliant on parents and other professionals for their interpretations of children's ideas and feelings.

Third, the time scales for completing the records, in particular initial assessments, were unrealistic – especially if the child had complex medical and educational needs and information had to be obtained from a number of professionals. Fourth, they expressed the concern that standardised forms rendered professional judgements more difficult, and were inappropriate for children whose development was not within the norms prescribed.

Discussion and implications for practice

This research was undertaken in the early stages of the implementation of the ICS. The problems identified with its use, as illustrated by this study, resulted in a series of consultations. In 2009 the Social Work Task Force recommended that an expert panel be set up to consult with local authorities on their use of the ICS. As a result local authorities have now been advised that their ICS systems should be:

> ...locally owned and locally implemented within a simplified national framework of guidance and specifications. (DCSF 2009b)

A number of strategic guides have been set up and local authorities now have or are in the process of redesigning and simplifying the exemplars to suit their local needs and those of their client population. In relation to involving children in recording, especially those with disabilities, simpler, fewer and better designed records should encourage social workers to enable the children they are working with to participate in their assessments, interventions and recording.

Children and their carers need to know what is being recorded and how

Even taking into account that this research was carried out during the early stages of the ICS implementation, a striking finding is that the children and their carers had not been informed about this new recording system and would not have been aware of it other than by involvement in this research project. This suggests that many young people have little meaningful and productive contact with their records – electronic or otherwise.

All children need to know what records are kept about them, what recording systems are in place and who has access to them.

Social workers need support and training in using computers, and should all be provided with a laptop to use outside the office

Many children have access to a computer, are knowledgeable about and comfortable with electronic communication. Social workers should be provided with laptops to use on home visits, and given information and training to engage children in their social work, including through computer-mediated communication, such as Viewpoint. However, face-to-face contact is still essential to establish a relationship of trust.

Clearly more evaluations of computer-assisted one-to-one communication is needed to determine in which situations technology can encourage children's involvement in recording.

Social workers need to be trained to communicate with children with disabilities

The disability substudy evidenced the need for social workers to be trained in and to have the time to use a range of communication skills to engage with children with disabilities, and to enable pictures and symbols to be filed as part of the record. Computers can be modified to operate in different ways to facilitate communication, especially for deaf and blind young people.

Children and their carers need to be involved in recording

Research suggests a pattern of recording, be it paper or electronic, which does not encourage children's participation nor lead them to see the possible benefits.

Social workers' training and policy directives need to encourage them to involve children in assessments and decisions, and to ensure that children contribute to and sign their records as an indication of their involvement, understanding and agreement.

Social workers need more time to undertake the direct work that will lead to children's engagement in recording. This means that case loads need to be smaller to free up time and that funding should be made available for training and support.

Establishing a meaningful relationship with the child is essential, based on active listening, respect and positive planning

Key to participatory practice is the practitioner's skill in forging a meaningful relationship. Social workers need to be trained and supported in developing their skills in direct work.

Supervision must focus on the social worker's ability to communicate with children, including through technology, and to enable them to exercise their right to contribute to and see their records at all stages of the process, from assessment to review. Writing the child's wishes and views into the records communicates that these have been taken seriously.

Recording systems need to be flexible

The study raised issues of format and design. The ICS tick box structure and inflexibility made the narrative hard to follow; the standardised forms made the many and complex needs of children with disabilities difficult to record; negative and judgemental terminology was off-putting.

Agencies now have permission to restructure their record systems to fit their local needs and to match the needs of different groups of children. There should be fewer and simpler forms. The language should be user friendly and accessible. Clear spaces should be created for children to indicate their wishes and responses. Managers should check all records have been signed by the child.

IT resources need to be provided

Children's services need to ensure their staff are computer literate and are aware of the tools and resources that are available for working with children on-line. IT specialists will need to be employed and should be responsive to practitioners' experiences of the systems that are put in place.

Agency culture

The culture of the employing agencies needs to reflect the role and values of social work that support the rights of children to participate, rather than a form-driven, procedural and mechanical system ill adapted to individual needs.

To promote and support participatory practice, the culture needs to reflect a tradition where the social work values are based on relationship rather than being enveloped by procedures and heavily bureaucratised tools of practice.

CHAPTER 9

Children's Views on their Involvement in Service Evaluation and Design

The R U Being Heard Project

'I think that most of social services do listen but a lot of them just think that we are little children who should be seen and not heard.' (16-year-old girl)

This chapter has a different focus in that it explores children's involvement in service evaluation and design, as well as how service providers respond to what children and young people say about the services they receive. It reports upon a study which explored how one authority evaluated and monitored the mechanisms it had in place for listening to young people's views and experiences of children's services in the statutory and voluntary sector, and their experience of this (Bell and Wilson 2002).

A decade ago, the involvement of children and young people in the design, planning and evaluation of services lagged behind their inclusion in individual decision making. After 2001 New Labour, through the Children and Young People's Unit, reinforced their commitment to children and young people to have more opportunities to get involved in the design, provision and evaluation of policies and services that affect them or which they use. Under New Labour this aspect of children's participation was substantially developed.

The work of the children's department described here, when the research was commissioned, provides a good example of how authorities were beginning to develop a wider range of ways of encouraging children's participation in their organisation's service delivery, as well as some of the difficulties. The city already had in place a number of organisations and activities which canvassed the views of children and young people. For example, they had conducted surveys, such as the Care Leavers Interview, where the views of young people leaving care were fed into a 20-point corrective action plan, specifying action the authority should take.

They also set up a process for involving looked-after young people in the recruitment and selection of staff for residential care homes. This compared favourably with the findings from the report, *Listen Then Commission* (Fry 2003), which found that only a few young people in the authorities they surveyed had been actively involved in the recruitment and training of foster carers, although they felt they had much to contribute, as has already been mentioned.

Further initiatives to facilitate the feedback of young people's views included their piloting the Viewpoint software, a computer programme. The complaints procedure for young people had also recently been revised following the upgrading of the complaints officer to the senior management group. A hotline to the assistant director provided children with access to senior management. This ensured that complaints were taken beyond the individual level and that the feedback was also given to the Area Child Protection Committee and to team managers. Clear time scales and the use of advocates from a voluntary agency ensured that the young people knew what had happened as a result of their complaint.

The work of the independent reviewing officers also evidenced a strong commitment to children's participation in conferences and reviews. Reviewing officers were proactive in preparing children for reviews by using new child-friendly review forms which had been designed in consultation with a children's group. Before the review, children were offered a choice of whether to speak on their own before it and/or to attend all or part of it.

Organisations in the voluntary sector also made a significant contribution to developing children's participation. One organisation, for example, provided a range of opportunities for young people to discuss, feed back and influence decision making in education and youth offending issues. Voluntary agencies also provided support to the children's department by assisting with the involvement of young people in recruiting staff – as described above. One hosted an open forum in an attempt to offer practitioners a monthly opportunity to discuss issues or differences of opinion.

Feedback systems from this voluntary organisation were rigorous: young people got copies of all correspondence sent out on their behalf; the agency accepted reverse charge calls, and were rigorous in reporting back from consultation events. The agency supported its own staff by providing structured and regular supervision, and was represented on a number of inter-agency committees. Their work exemplifies a range of strengths in participatory practice. The agency is rooted in a culture of children's rights, and their policy and practice flow from this strong value base. Young people are closely involved in many of their group activities, such as the one described above, which provided a model for review meetings.

Agencies in the voluntary sector also undertook reactive work. For example, responses were made to issues brought by the young people – notably work with schools on non-attendance and anti-bullying. Advocacy services were provided for a range of situations, including for young people in residential care where regular visits were made and for children who were complaining. An Independent Visitors scheme was progressing the use of advocacy. Other initiatives in response to local need included projects such as using Diana money (from the Princess Diana Trust) to set up outreach work with asylum seekers, and joint work with the Children's Centre to facilitate consultation with disabled children.

A national voluntary agency in the city also had schemes for developing opportunities for young people with disabilities to consult and feedback their comments in newsletters which were also sent to families. The work of their multi-agency working group was at the core of their involvement with young people, with professionals working closely together on corporate planning and specific partnership groups, as well as with individual families. Consultation projects, such as that on transport facilities in the city, took forward very practical issues identified by families. The activity project funded by the Children's Fund, described above, involved taking young people away on holiday for two weeks to help them to express their views about the services they received. This evidenced a real attempt to engage the young people themselves.

So, while the local authority had a number of structures and initiatives in place for progressing the participation agenda – especially by funding developments in the voluntary sector – it was aware that, to progress the agenda further, the mechanisms in place in the statutory agencies involved could be more effective. This stage of development could be defined as being at the second stage of Wright and Haydon's (2002) four stages. They suggested that participatory practice in organisations takes place first by establishing a commitment to participation, and second by planning and developing participative ways of working. The latter stages would involve setting up structures for assessing change, developing practice and setting up reviews. This chapter takes forward our knowledge of the factors that can both facilitate and get in the way of service responses to children's expressed views.

The study

The study was commissioned by an authority in the north of England in 2002. The main issues which they invited the researchers (Bell and Wilson) to explore were:

- to clarify exactly what was in place, and to gather information about any potential for overlap in the existing listening mechanisms and feedback loops

- to explore the representation from groups who were socially excluded, in particular children from black and ethnic minority groups and looked-after children

- to evaluate the systems in place for using the information gathered from children to inform planning and decision making, and to explore ways of feeding it back into practice and training.

Additionally, the authority wished to know, from the children and young people, what listening meant to them and whether they believed that what they said was heard and had any effect on the services they received as individuals or on the broader base of planning and delivery of services. And, from the statutory and externally commissioned services, how practitioners and managers conceived their role in listening to and responding to young people.

The overall aims of the study were therefore:

- to ascertain the views of the key stakeholders – the children and the professionals – about the existing mechanisms for listening and responding to children

- to produce a view as to how the tasks, processes and systems were being experienced by all involved, and managed by the authority.

Method

To elicit the views of a range of young people, questionnaires were sent to three groups of children aged between 6 and 19; children who were looked after, children in receipt of services for children in need and children attending voluntary agencies. The questionnaire was designed to provide information about who the children had talked to, what information they were given and whether things changed as a result. It was supplemented by a focus group and in-depth interviews with a small number of children.

The views of the professionals on their role in listening to and responding to children, the skills and support they considered necessary and the effectiveness or otherwise of the systems in place were obtained in telephone interviews. Those approached included practitioners, managers and assistant directors from all sectors and levels of children's services and from a range of voluntary agencies.

The sample

THE CHILDREN

Seventy-six young people responded to the questionnaire, their ages ranging from 6 to 19, with a mean age of 13.19. Over half were girls, and 98 per cent were white European. The largest group comprised young people who were looked after (42%). Thirty-four of the respondents were in contact with the social services department and the remainder with other agencies such as Youth Offending, and voluntary agencies such as Barnado's and Kingfisher.

THE PROFESSIONALS

Twenty-eight professionals from the statutory and voluntary sector, from basic grade to director level, were interviewed.

Findings

The children's views

Two thirds of the children were in contact with a social worker. Opinions varied as to their 'helpfulness', nearly half finding them very helpful, a third sometimes helpful and a few never helpful (see Table 9.1). From an 11-year-old boy:

> 'I did have a social worker called X but I have not seen him for four months – can I have a new one please?'

The girls were less positive than the boys, and the 'never helpfuls' were all aged 13 or over and more likely to be female.

Table 9.1 How helpful do you find it to see your social worker?

	Number of children	Percentage
Very helpful	22	43
Sometimes helpful	18	35
Never helpful	4	8
Don't know	7	14
Total	51	100

The picture from children with disabilities (N=8) was of a dearth of social work contact, and of greater use, instead, of other workers, such as community nurse, teacher and Barnardo's. Of those who had contact with workers from the voluntary sector there was a strong preference for that worker. From a boy aged 9:

> 'I don't think my social workers who keep changing listen to me but my other helpers listen carefully and help where they can.'

The most common topic was problems at school, ranging from specific accounts of serious bullying, to more general issues about 'school arrangements'. Another prominent area was 'family'. Most of the looked-after young people mentioned concerns about contact with family members. From a 6-year-old girl:

> 'We talked about when we can go back to Mummy and Daddy, and how to see Grandpa.'

They also mentioned everyday affairs of importance to them, such as clothes, pocket money and bedtime arrangements, but also court, care and 'what I've been up to and what I have done in the past' (11-year-old girl). This was in contrast to young people living at home who were more likely to mention activities, school, friends, 'who I go out with', and 'belly button piercing'.

A number, similar to those involved in child protection investigations, used their time with their social worker to reflect upon their own behaviour: 'offences committed and ways of changing my behaviour' (13-year-old boy); 'about a behaviour chart and moving to live with B and S' (8-year-old boy). More generally, discussions about feelings included 'the past' and 'why I don't wanna know my family' (16-year-old boy).

Also echoing the children in Chapter 7, older children were concerned about the future:

> 'She [social worker] normally asks me when you're older would you like to live on your own or in a hostel – because she helps me to know [what I] really want.'

A few, more particularly young people with disabilities, mentioned college, further education or 'advice'. From a boy aged 16:

> '…about how I would like to go for respite with other children like me but there is nowhere I am able to go.'

Apart from their social workers, the amount of contact with other professionals varied. Seventy-six per cent found it very easy or easy to find someone to talk to, teachers featuring most prominently with 35 per cent rating them as very helpful. Twenty-five mentioned learning support, their experience generally being positive. Doctors and school nurses were mentioned less frequently, regarded mainly as being 'sometimes helpful' and consulted on specific health issues. Some said they would 'never talk to a doctor or school nurse about private things'.

Where contact with voluntary agencies was mentioned they were found to be very helpful, engendering a sense of empowerment and companionship. Contact with a residential worker or foster carer was also generally found helpful. Thirty-five of the respondents said they talked with people close to them, naming family – parents, siblings, grandparents and friends. Others mentioned included family support worker, community nurse, helpline, psychiatrist, drug support and school mentors.

The concerns shared with this group of professionals were generally similar to those discussed with social workers. Again, bullying in school and harassment took prominence:

> 'It was all about the bullying and harassment and threats.' (17-year-old girl)

The qualities of approachability, accessibility and relationship were mentioned for all professional contacts. The right kind of manner (not patronising), attitude and being treated with respect and taken seriously were considered important.

Regarding trust, comments included: 'I feel close to these people' and 'felt they were my friends'.

Regarding accessibility: 'because they are there and always want to listen when someone's in need' (13-year-old girl) and 'I knew who would be there for me if I need them' (16-year-old girl).

Listening behaviours received frequent mention, as did confidentiality and straightforward language. From a girl aged 17:

> 'If I'm talking about my feelings it's just better for them to listen instead of putting on the "Mr Fix It Hat".'

What happened next was important, especially knowing that something would happen as a result of the discussion:

> 'It helps when sometimes he can sort out problems for me.'

> 'They stopped the bullies picking on me.'

Practical arrangements, such as 'helping with school attendance officer' were noted. The children quickly sussed who could help, and a number said suggesting strategies, for example dealing with bullying, was helpful. They found it hard when they were unsure what help was available, relationships were unfamiliar or people seemed too busy. They also worried about the repercussions of disclosing information, as expressed by this 12-year-old girl:

> 'If you told that someone had punched you then it may happen again because you have told.'

RESPONDING

We asked the children what they thought might happen next. Most (90%) found the information they had been given easy to understand. Fifty-two per cent said they were told a lot about what would happen, while 28 per cent said a little and the remaining 20 per cent said they were not told or could not remember. Eighty-two per cent said that they were told about their 'rights', and 79 per cent that they had been told something about how to complain.

Nine of the children, all in some form of residential provision, mainly female and aged over 13, had made formal complaints. Two were positive about what had happened, it was 'brilliant – more effective than talking to them social workers', and were satisfied with the outcome. For the others, such as the 16-year-old girl quoted at the beginning of this chapter, there was a desire that more should happen and change as a result of what they had told social services and that their views could be taken more seriously.

Over 80 per cent of the young people said they were asked what they wanted to happen. Two thirds said their views were written down and that they were listened to in reviews and meetings. From an 11-year-old girl:

> 'They respect my opinion and discuss my views and try to help me explain myself properly.'

A number, such as this 10-year-old boy, expressed greater confidence in talking to friends or other professionals:

> 'Social services don't tell the full truth at all. I've got more confidence in friends.'

Fifty-seven per cent said their views were acted upon, and, generally views were positive – that things were being done and did change. Most of the negative views were from young people who were looked after, reporting that their wishes in relation to placement choice were not met. One respondent suggested that action only happened if others saw it as important. However, a third of all young people said not enough was done. Some suggestions related to specific situations: 'The headmaster could have done more and my head of year' (16-year-old girl). More generally, the advice was to listen, understand and respond to wishes and feelings: 'People should have listened and seen how hard it was' (15-year-old girl). One suggestion, from a 13-year-old boy, was to disseminate information about where support can be found:

> 'Yes, if posters and cards were put around schools, college, pub, Stagecoach canteen, on buses, trains, taxi ranks and police stations.'

The professionals' views

Of the 28 professionals interviewed from the statutory and voluntary sector, all expressed awareness of their own and their agency's role in listening and responding to children's concerns, though there were differences of emphasis depending on their role and their agency's function:

- Principal Social Workers emphasised duties: 'We have a duty to listen to children and provide systems for responding – at the heart of Quality Protects.'

- Managers emphasised rights: 'Children and young people have a right to be heard and consulted.'

- Practitioners emphasised roles and the responsibility of their agency: 'Our role is to listen to them, advocate for them; ensure information is provided…it can be difficult.'

Most respondents had some direct contact with children. Principals and managers maintained indirect contact through committee membership, meetings, initiatives and consultation events, and saw these opportunities as vital in shaping the direction of the services, and sometimes in instilling more urgency into policy making:

'We should be more involved as managers in our position and should meet these groups – empowering for those groups and extremely helpful for us – can bypass about six months of planning – you hear it and it can cut through all the…'

Some practitioners in the statutory services wished for more time to spend with children in contrast to practitioners in the voluntary agencies who had a lot of contact: 'Our work is 100 per cent one to one.'

In relation to children with disabilities, concern was expressed that contact was generally with families, rather then directly with the children. However, developmental work was being undertaken to find more effective ways for providing children with disabilities with a forum of their own.

LISTENING

Most of the professionals thought opportunities for listening were in place and that practice was developing. They were aware that consulting and listening to children's views was a statutory requirement, and were knowledgeable about the frameworks in place to support the policy and practice of active listening. Social service respondents thought the statutory procedures provided a sound and varied structure for children's views to be sought and recorded, citing reviews, child protection case conferences, LAC reports and care plans, social worker records, Regulation 22 visits, statements to the courts, and the complaints procedure. However, the use of these formal structures was patchy and not always effective. The voluntary agencies were used effectively to help the authority in this work, and, as described above, had systems in place outside statutory mechanisms for hearing children's views. However, there was concern that many of the volunteers were untrained.

Particular difficulties were identified with certain groups such as children in foster care, children with disabilities and unaccompanied refugee children. The views of black and minority ethnic children were rarely mentioned except by the director responsible for developing this work, and a leaflet had been designed to reach these groups. There was also recognition that broader concerns should be responded to other than on an individual basis.

A number of impediments to effective listening were highlighted. These included a lack of the facilities available for social workers to engage with children, and a falling off in direct work with children in certain areas, for example in life story work, because of lack of time or confidence on the part of practitioners. The volume of paperwork meant practitioners had little time. It was often the least experienced practitioners who had most opportunity for listening to children, yet they lacked the necessary skill and confidence.

A number of the managers defined the problem as being 'cultural... some see children's rights as a threat'. Concern was expressed that some basic 'core professional skills' were being eroded or insufficiently supported and encouraged. The supports needed to enable practitioners to listen included team support and good supervision, time and facilities. Managers stressed the importance of review and appraisal and training, especially in relation to attitudes and the need for a culture shift.

RESPONDING

All of the respondents felt that young people's views were not accorded enough weight: 'we're not there yet', and 'it's patchy'. Reasons given were either internal to the organisation – that the culture needs to change – or external – that the barriers were endemic to the job:

> 'Realistically we can't always do what the child wants – part of the professional role is to balance wishes with needs.'

Gaining consent from foster carers to talk to a young person provides another example of the complexity of the ethical issues involved. Lack of provision was a further reason given for not responding to the young person's views. For example, in residential care:

> 'The resources are not there for really attending to what a young person wants, if, say, it's for a foster placement and to leave a residential unit.'

It was acknowledged, also, that skills varied in managing these tensions:

> 'We do need to communicate and explain to the child why something is or isn't being done – sometimes we dodge this…sometimes we try and are not heard.'

The professionals thought that, while progress was being made, there was no system in place for pulling out themes or aggregating views:

> 'Current structures don't always ensure that children are responded to – it has become a divided responsibility and sometimes feels as if no one is properly keeping an eye on it all.'

One suggestion was to distinguish between those situations where the systems for individual responses were working well but resources were inadequate – as with foster placements, the Independent Visitors scheme, or with the befriending services – and systems for bringing together information so that themes can be identified:

> 'This may be occurring at management level, but there is a lack of transparency and communication and feedback down the line.'

Comments were then made on the use of records, such as LAC forms, in eliciting and gathering information about children's views. The view, generally, was that while records and forms might provide evidence that a young person's views had been sought, they were not necessarily effective as tools for communicating with young people. In some cases information was not recorded because of difficulties around confidentiality (especially for young people in foster care), balancing a young person's needs against concerns of adults, fear of giving false reassurance and time pressures. A voluntary project manager commented that although evaluation forms were kept, and there was a 12-week review system of individual contacts, there was no systematic way of feeding these evaluations back into the policy and practice of the project.

The complaints procedure, described above, was seen to model an effective and well-developed structure for response at an individual level. However, it was said that few complaints progressed beyond Stage 1:

> 'The effort is put into making the complaint go away, rather than allowing things to develop into planning and policy. If children were allowed to run bullying to Stage 2 the department would have to be more responsive.'

Again, it was felt that, while the outcome for individuals was clear, 'patterns are not pulled together'.

Providing evidence of a growing culture of openness and willingness to consult young users, both statutory and voluntary agencies were involved in a number of initiatives where the views of young people on their services were sought. Examples included a drama group for asylum seekers and a disco for looked-after children which included consultation about their perspectives. The Corporate Anti-bullying Strategy is an example of a multi-agency plan to address bullying, supported through training initiatives. Youth Offending Teams (YOTs) provided some examples of good practice in working closely with teachers and young people on problems in school. However, the evidence from the young people suggested that practice was variable and the strategy was not always implemented effectively. There was a general view that the rhetoric of consultation outpaced the reality – especially from the social services department:

> 'Some groups become very bureaucratic – the conferences are well attended, but exactly what comes out and how we get these recommendations fed back into policy and practice is sometimes quite difficult – whatever is the flavour is picked up.'

MONITORING SYSTEMS FOR RESPONDING

Clearly, monitoring of the systems for responding is key to their transparency and development. There was some evidence of monitoring by managers and principals, for example in residential homes by independent monthly rota visits, and by follow-up action plans, but the corrective action process was patchy.

> 'There are still loose ends and not all feedback loops are closed.'

At practitioner level, audits of a sample of records took place monthly. Independent reviewing officers audit all review plans, although much of the interaction is verbal. Additionally, staff appraisal provided opportunities for identifying training and value issues.

It was felt that practitioners were primarily responsible for their own records, and that managers and principals encouraged being 'the champions' of the cause.

> 'Part of our overall strategy is to identify champions [of children] and then be sure they're given back-up. It's an organic process – we engender a culture of openness, putting like-minded people together.'

Overall, most respondents felt that the systems for responding and monitoring lacked co-ordination at systems, agency and practitioner levels. There was concern that 'they're tokenistic – is it real participation?', that they lacked cohesion and that there was no strategic planning:

> 'It's all problem focused – energy goes into day-to-day issues, with no feedback loops. We respond to the same problem over and over again, but don't address the issues that cause it; it's neither preventive nor corrective.'

At the same time there was concern about bureaucratising the process of responding:

> 'Management systems are invented to keep kids at bay. There's simply not enough manpower on the ground.'

ADVOCACY

Respondents commented on the wide range of advocacy schemes, emphasising the role of voluntary organisations as offering a broad range, including campaigning, educational, young men's, young women's, and parents' groups. While principals and managers said that advocacy was provided when children needed it, the views of practitioners were more mixed. Some regarded themselves as having a significant role as advocating for the child in meetings. Others used advocates from voluntary organisations. The work of the volunteers scheme in providing advocacy was often invisible to other agencies, and difficulties in managing a volunteers service, with the need to balance numbers and neither over- or under-recruit volunteers was mentioned.

The use of advocacy in the complaints procedure was seen as effective in encouraging children and young people to complain and in ensuring they had independent representation and support. The need to expand advocacy services was expressed, especially for children in settings such as family group conferences. There was disagreement about the role of Children's Guardians as advocates, some thinking they had an important advocacy role while others disagreed. Knowledge of and experience of Independent Visitors was varied and there had been a problem of availability.

THE DIFFICULTIES

Some areas were identified as being particularly complex, including children in foster care, in residential care and children with disabilities. Again, the barriers were seen as arising from the culture:

> 'The customer is the child, not the foster carer...we need to do some refocusing training so they sense a child piggybacking them and whispering in their ear "find me a good placement".'

Tensions were felt to be endemic to the situation:

> 'From the carers' point of view what do we do with the information the children give us – what should be shared?... There's some tension here.'

In residential care, staff were concerned at being on the end of a complaint and were therefore on the defensive. However, here, also, developments have been instituted, such as residents meetings where the information is logged and then taken to the staff meeting. Again, a voluntary agency was used to mediate internal disputes. Children with disabilities were highlighted as needing particular input:

> 'We're at the beginning of a long road – other children are being consulted to death but we're just starting.'

Another theme identified as contributing to the difficulty in enabling children to participate was the lack of a unified system for co-ordinating and mapping inter-agency relationships. The rapid development of a plethora of short-term projects and initiatives had intensified the problem.

The difficulties in co-ordination included paradoxically both a dearth of meetings, and so many meetings there is no time for anything else. Although a range of meetings and groups were in place to provide opportunities for inter-agency contact, some commented they were 'not clear what happens as a result'. Inter-agency contact was felt to have become bureaucratised, with little contact with children, and a worry that the same young people were getting help from them all.

The role of voluntary agencies was clearly recognised in developing projects in response to need, in providing advocacy and independent representation, in filling gaps and in putting pressure on statutory agencies to be more responsive. At the same time it was felt that their development needed stabilising, that, in relation to their role in providing advocacy, there was a blurring of roles which needed clarifying and that their involvement in contentious issues could be seen as adversarial. Further, that it could create a splitting process whereby young people regarded them as all good and statutory workers as all bad.

Problems in contacts with the voluntary sector arose from difficulties in sharing information about specific cases, and about policy decisions where funding was required. Quarterly meetings were held to review mechanisms for working together, but were only partly satisfactory. The service level agreement established several years ago needed updating and the recognition of joint responsibility re-emphasising. A suggestion was for a single line management structure, delivered through an independent body:

> 'So they're all reporting to the same people, there's some synergy between them, and they're all singing to the same song sheet.'

Discussion and implications for practice

This study is wider in scope than those described in the earlier studies. It did not attempt to measure the numbers of children consulted in service planning. Neither did it analyse statistics relating to, for example, attendance at statutory reviews or the numbers of care plans signed by young people. As is clear from earlier chapters, research on such involvement does not necessarily imply young people's participation;

likewise, research on the core assessment documents, for example, suggests that counting ticks is not a reliable way of demonstrating children's participation in their assessment or review.

The research reported here described the views of 76 children and 28 staff involved in the business of providing opportunities for children in need to be listened to, heard and responded to. Taken together, the responses of the children and the professionals clarify what systems are in place for children's participation and describe what children and the staff involved think of them. Although coming from different standpoints, the consistency between the two groups is striking. Both highlight areas which they find work well, especially in the mechanisms available for listening and consulting. Both also highlight areas where work is needed, mostly concerning how children's views are responded to, and how changes as a result of their views are fed back into the system.

Formal monitoring and evaluation measures need to be in place

This authority reflects a common pattern: while participation was regarded as a key 'target', monitoring and formal evaluation procedures were limited – meaning that policy changes were unlikely to result. The systems need to be sufficiently robust to identify general themes and to promote corrective action into service planning and delivery.

A senior manager or group could construct a system for codifying the concerns and prioritise what it is possible, practicable and achievable to tackle. Strategies for participation need to be consistent, and linked with an action plan to put in place robust systems for pulling together concerns that are identified in individual cases in the different sectors.

The outcomes of projects should be reviewed. Specific gaps or areas for improvement should be identified and named.

The processes of involving young people in policy planning and delivery require organisational change, especially in relation to culture and practice

Progress in involving young people in policy planning and delivery is slow and should happen at all levels of the organisation – from senior management down to frontline staff. A 'whole systems' approach needs to be in place across the four levels of culture, structure, practice and effective review (see Wright *et al.* 2006). Changing the culture is necessary so that it is child-centred and collaborative.

Information about existing and proposed activities should be shared across agencies. Voluntary agencies can have a key role and their funding should continue. In this study they placed user involvement at the core of their activity, and held regular meetings where young people were involved in taking decisions about initiatives.

Where events happen clear action must result and be fed back to the children so that they do not appear to be tokenistic.

The authority needs to be clear what they want to change, to develop a participation strategy and to produce a mission statement built upon children's rights

Organisational culture reflects the values that underpin practice and plays a key role in facilitating the response to young people's views. Authorities need to be clear what they want to change. They should develop a participation strategy and produce a mission statement built upon children's rights and identifying good practice.

The mission statement would draw upon the perspectives of the young people and identify avenues for promoting user involvement. It should propose clear plans as to how information will be fed back into the planning process and how the participation strategy will be implemented by each agency.

Children can offer valuable comment on structural issues, such as changing the image of children's services and encouraging the dissemination of information about available services. They can also suggest action on specific issues – such as changes of worker, and contact arrangements.

All organisations should establish a multi-agency group with responsibility for implementing strategies for taking into account children's views, and each agency should identify a children's champion

Each agency should identify a champion, a catalyst for change, who would involve all staff and promote partnership activities across health, education and the voluntary sector. This should be a person who children trust, who could advocate for them, and who ensures issues regarding rights and participation are 'kept alive'.

A corporate participation strategy, built upon children's rights, and identifying good practice in listening and responding should be developed and agreed by every agency, including a mission statement drawing upon the perspectives of the children and young people themselves.

The establishment of an executive multi-agency group responsible for the implementation of the strategy is also indicated, alongside the setting up of a Children's Rights Service.

A listening and responding team could be set up to develop training, and to plan and integrate the development of participatory practice with the voluntary agencies

The study emphasises the importance of developing and learning new ways of working with young people. Since good social work practice underpins effective participation, resources need to be provided to support practitioners in direct work with children, for example by structuring teams comprising practitioners with different specialist skills.

A task force could be set up to recommend strategies for training and co-ordination across teams and sectors, and to develop the infrastructure.

Children's positive experience with staff at all levels promotes their engagement

Echoing findings from the other studies, where the children's experiences had been positive, their engagement – and hence the opportunity to progress their participation in the social work process – was enhanced. Social workers need to have the time to be physically and emotionally available to the children on their case loads and to listen and help without taking over.

The role of voluntary agencies was important, as was the role teachers played in, for example, bullying. Addressing children's personal problems in a particular setting might connect with engagement in wider policy issues, in this case, with consultation in schools on anti-bullying policies.

The views of all children need to be taken seriously and responded to, even if their wishes cannot be met

Children valued having information about what would happen next, their rights and how to complain – and experience of making complaints was generally positive. Most said they had been asked what they wanted to happen. Taking their views seriously was important. A format should be developed for feeding back to young people how the agency is tackling issues raised at a policy level. This would place the solution where it belongs, and not individualise it.

Particular care needs to be taken of children who 'fall through the net', such as unaccompanied minors and children from ethnic minority groups. There is a need to develop ways of communicating with younger children and children with disabilities.

Access to independent advocacy and other services is important

Independent advocacy services, widely cited as being of value, should continue to be supported and developed. The role of voluntary agencies is key in promoting service development and delivery – particularly in relation to independent advocacy – and service level agreements with key voluntary agencies should reflect the need for developing participatory services together.

Access to independent advocacy is an important safeguard for young people who consider their views and experiences of services are not recognised.

Up-to-date and accurate information about what is available in the area is essential. In order to enable professionals to know what is available to support children's participation, there should be a database comprising a directory of existing service provision in different service areas. This would provide information for both professionals and service users on a range of services (including training packs) and enable the identification of gaps in provision.

CHAPTER 10

Implications for Practice

The studies described in earlier chapters have provided graphic illustrations of children's experiences of involvement in different types of social work meetings, in social work recording systems and of consultation within a children's department. The children's experiences vary; some are positive, others negative and some mixed. Certainly, children's participation in social work decision making and organisational issues is not always easy but it is essential to promote. What these studies and others point up is that where children have participated they are more likely to have engaged in the process of change, their confidence and self esteem can be heightened and their involvement can lead to better and more responsive services.

In this chapter I will pull together the main findings from the studies before laying out the implications for practice.

Overview of the studies

The findings from the studies have much in common. Whatever the context, be it a frightening child protection conference, involvement in their social work records or more general consultation about service provisions, what comes up time and again is that children's experiences of participation depend upon their relationship with the adults who are working with them. Common to all the research studies reported in the previous chapters is the key role of the child's social worker in promoting participatory practice and, linked to that, the culture of the agency in supporting these values and facilitating the child's involvement in the various decision-making processes. Children in all the studies reported describe the features of relationship, practice and organisational culture that enable them to exercise their right to be included, to express their views and to engage in the transaction.

The children in the family group conferences valued the opportunity to talk in depth about their family and to ask questions. Discussions were generally productive, and enabled some of the children to develop insights into their own behaviour. They disliked feeling silenced, victimised and unsupported, and were more likely to experience distress or conflicting loyalties when the social worker or convener was not present.

In the child protection study the children engaged in the transaction when they trusted their social worker and experienced her as a person who had a genuine interest in their lives, who could demonstrate that she related to them in an age-appropriate way and who offered them some degree of choice and control. They needed to feel safe and protected and that their social worker believed what they said and took them seriously. Even very young children were aware of having been given individual attention and listened to. In the words of Butler Sloss (cited in the Cleveland Report 1988), they were treated as persons, not as objects.

What they experienced as unhelpful was going over old ground which re-activated painful experiences. They realised this may be necessary for adult understanding – especially where their social workers changed, and the professional network was being expanded – but this reinforced their sense that the agenda was not theirs. Where they became aware that professionals were party to detailed information about their lives which they had not given they felt out of control. Where concern seemed to be 'turned on' they felt infantilised. When their views were not respected or acted upon they felt betrayed. Careful preparation for meetings, including of their preferred representation, was necessary.

The young people in the ICS study also knew what they wanted from their social worker: to be listened to, respected and to have outcomes that enhanced their lives. And they wanted results: housing, health and education – and planning to go home for those in care. They also spoke most favourably of the interpersonal aspects of service provision, such as the amount of time spent with their social worker and the extent to which they felt they were being understood and listened to. For these young people, as with those in the other studies, the most important thing was their relationship with their social worker, and some concrete outcomes of their choosing. However, their views were not recorded on the ICS forms, about which they knew nothing. And the social workers did not find the ICS system promoted children's involvement in recording.

In the local authority study, listening behaviours again received frequent mention, as did confidentiality and straightforward language. Approachability and accessibility was valued, as was being treated with respect. The children needed to know that something would happen and valued practical arrangements. Regarding their involvement in wider issues, voluntary agencies were important. The role teachers played in bullying was stressed, providing an example of how addressing children's personal problems in a particular setting might connect with engagement in wider policy issues, in this case with consultation in schools on anti-bullying policies.

In this study the most negative experiences echoed those in the other studies – a sense of disillusionment that what they said they wanted to happen could not be delivered, and that things didn't change. While such experiences were disempowering, the children had suggestions for action on specific issues, such as changes of worker, and contact arrangements. The agencies needed to create systems where these suggestions were tabled and responded to.

What works?

Now I will extract from the above some clear guidance for what promotes participatory practice. Although there are some differences in relation to the arena in which children are participating, be it individual social work or involvement in service delivery, it is striking that the qualities of effective practice, organisational culture and good management are very similar.

Principles and values

All work with children starts with the child at the centre. Agencies' policies and managers' and practitioners' values should be child-centred, democratic and collaborative.

- Keep the child in mind and make sense of the child's world.

- Respect the child as an individual with rights; all children should be valued.

- Children are competent and have agency; all should contribute to decisions.

- Children should be given choice and control; they are not victims.
- Social workers hold power; it must be used judiciously.
- Attitudes must be non-judgemental and holistic.

A value base grounded in these principles requires awareness of our own identity in terms of class, ethnicity, sexuality and disability, and of our own childhood. We need to be aware of how others see us and how we see others. Power is integral to the social work role and must be managed sensitively.

Organisational cultures should reflect these values. All organisations should base their policies, procedures and staff training and structures on a culture that is child-centred, including an understanding that it takes time to build trust and communicate effectively with children.

Safe practice

In all work with children practitioners will have the proper intention of protecting children from risk. This means that the child's voice has to be listened to, heard and responded to within the parameters of risk and safety.

Work with parents or carers will be necessary to ensure proper access is gained in a space in which the child feels safe. Organisations should ensure rooms and facilities are provided which enable individuals and groups to meet in privacy, with time and with appropriate resources. On home visits practitioners must ensure they see the child alone.

- All children must be seen alone, in privacy.
- The venue should be accessible and pleasant.
- What children don't say can be as important as what they do say; silence speaks volumes.
- Non-verbal communication must be seen and listened to, and should be taken as seriously as the spoken word.
- All children can contribute to assessment, recording, decision making and planning providing the means of communication is appropriate to their needs.
- Honesty about time, process and limitations is essential.
- There must be clear understanding relating to issues of confidentiality and consent from the start.

- All children should be kept informed of developments, with frequent checking that they have understood.

- The possible outcomes of any intervention need to be spelled out time and again, including explanations about what is possible or impossible.

Communication

The child must be seen alone and appropriate and creative ways of communication should be used and resources made available.

- Simple language is essential.

- For young children play work is essential.

- For some children, drawings, symbols or signing are their language.

- Exercises, role play and sculpting can be used.

- Computer-assisted communication programmes can be helpful.

- Websites and technology can facilitate communication.

Creating a relationship of trust

A child's capacity to participate requires that they trust the adults they are working with. A relationship of trust takes time to build and maintain – and that time should be protected, with the balance held between personal and professional skills. A meaningful relationship is based on always listening to the voice of the child, taking the child seriously and responding to his wishes and feelings – even where his wishes cannot be fulfilled (De Boer and Coady 2007). The skill is to balance and continually negotiate and renegotiate with children, and to provide space where they can think for themselves.

Personal qualities are:

- availability: physical and emotional

- attitude: treating children as individuals, with respect

- attunement: active listening and appropriate responses

- kindness: being supportive and companionable

- providing safe boundaries

- awareness of one's power.

Professional qualities are:

- continuity of care
- reliability and availability
- setting ground rules and forming written working agreements
- making all information accessible
- promoting self care skills
- providing concrete help
- being clear and honest
- offering genuine choice and distinctive options; encouraging the child to own the work
- good, collaborative record keeping and storage
- giving feedback.

Stopping children falling through the net

All the studies revealed that particular attention has to be paid to children who are socially excluded such as unaccompanied minors, children from ethnic minority groups and children with disabilities. It should not be assumed that younger children are unable to express a view or participate in decision making.

- A range of communication skills need to be developed and used.
- For children who don't speak English careful choice of and work with interpreters is necessary.
- Where parents do not speak English, children need to be relieved of the responsibility of translating for them.
- Trained workers and facilities are needed for children with disabilities.

Preparing children for key events

Whatever the arena, there will be times or events where key decisions are made. Children need careful preparation for these.

- Information should be provided in a way and at a time that the child or group can take it in.
- Preparation includes:

- ◦ describing the process of what happens next, and providing leaflets

- ◦ discussing what an assessment comprises, and the process of assessment through to review and what the hoped-for outcomes are

- ◦ outlining possible interventions, including limitations

- ◦ offering genuine choice, for example who they would like to be at a meeting or event.

- • Careful records need to be kept, and children need to know where they are stored and who has access to them.

- • Children need to know what resources and interventions are available.

- • Feedback, and checking out understanding on an ongoing basis is essential.

Most appropriate representation

In considering the most appropriate means of a child's participation social workers need to discuss this with the child beforehand and exercise professional judgement.

- • Considering the child's physical presence is the starting point.

- • There may be contra-indications to the child's physical presence.

- • Scripts can be written or drawn; tapes or videos can be created.

- • Advocates can be offered and worked with.

- • Interpreters can be found, briefed and supported.

- • In group situations the representative should reflect the views of all.

The management of meetings

Meetings need to be child friendly, informal and, where possible, small. Care needs to be taken of who is invited, where they are held and that the agenda reflects the child's concerns.

- • Information should be provided before a meeting, and constantly clarified. It should be:

- ◦ about the issues to be aired

- tailored to address the child's concerns.
- The child's permission should be gained before confidential information is shared, and careful explanations given if confidentiality has to be breached.
- The chairperson should ensure the child's voice is heard, for example by having an agenda item entitled 'views of the child'.
- Where children's wishes cannot be met, they need to know and understand the reasons. Openness and honesty are essential.
- Private time needs careful thought and management.
- Continuing support from the key worker afterwards is important.

Organisational culture

Dynamic leadership, based on participatory values and principles, is necessary to promote and develop participatory practice in organisations.

- The leadership model should be collaborative, not hierarchical.
- Children should, where appropriate, set their own agenda, initiate actions and have a budget.
- Each Trust area should create a network of participation opportunities.
- Each Trust area should train and support partner agencies.
- Technology supports participation, particularly in policy making, and should be made available to all.
- Champions of children's rights or participation workers should be identified within each organisation, and provided with back-up.
- Trusts need to be clear what they want to change and to have in place systems that identify general themes leading to corrective action in service planning and delivery.
- A format for feeding back to the child or group how the agency has tackled issues at a policy level should be created.
- Evidence of the outcomes that have been achieved should be provided in writing.

Management and supervision of staff

Direct work with children should be prioritised. This means ensuring practitioners have sufficient time for every case they are allocated or project they are working on, and training should be appropriate and updated. Budgets should include the cost of resources, such as space, technology, refreshments, toys and play materials.

As well as time and facilities, practitioners need team support and good supervision to maintain the core professional skills that underpin participatory practice. This means:

- Supervision should be regular and timely. Reflective practice should be encouraged. Practitioners' feelings about the children they are working with should be addressed.

- Every case or event should be reviewed regularly.

- Regular staff and team appraisal needs to address case loads and developments.

- Training should address the need for attitudinal change, and enable skills and confidence in participatory practice to develop.

- Records and plans should be routinely audited to ensure the child's wishes and feelings are recorded, outcomes identified and that this has been communicated to the child.

CHAPTER 11

Conclusion

Both globally and within the UK children, by law, now have the right to have their say in a number of arenas. They are consulted on national and international political affairs, involved in decisions that are made within their local communities and schools and engaged in different aspects of their social work. While children's participation in all of these arenas forms the context of the discussion in this book, the focus and illustrative studies are on the particularly complex arena of social work with vulnerable children.

The book began by defining what we mean by participation and exploring the arenas and spaces in which it takes place and the outcomes that can be achieved. We then looked at the different methods of children's participation, from physical presence to representation, advocacy and consultation. The discussion proceeded by tracking the development of policy and practice over the last three decades and explored how shifts in our conceptions about the care and protection of children have changed in the UK in response to a range of issues, including social and economic development and child abuse inquiries. This was followed by a critique of the theories that underpin participatory practice. Part I finished by exploring some of the ways in which adult attitudes have informed the theories and policies that have shaped the development of participatory practice with children.

Part II provided illustrations of children's participation by describing four research studies which illustrated the points made in Part I. Two described children's experiences of participating in meetings and reviews, the third their involvement in the electronic recording systems that social workers now use, and the fourth evaluated their experience of contributing to policy making in a children's department. Some of the issues that the research highlights centred on current policy, some on practice and some on the organisational management and culture of children's departments.

The issues arising are entwined. Social workers deliver and implement policy. Their capacity to effect the meaningful participation of children in their work depends upon their skills and knowledge, as well as the space, resources and support they have to make it effective. In turn, these capacities are largely determined by the culture of the organisations which social work inhabits, which themselves are driven by government policy, guidance and the consequent procedures, targets and performance indicators.

The previous chapter presented an overview from the studies of the children's experiences, and laid out the implications for practice arising for practitioners, their organisational culture and management. The children in all the studies talk about being listened to. What comes across is that the words 'listening to' can be interpreted differently. In interviewing young people, McLeod (2008) found that while the social workers said they did listen to looked-after children (i.e. they heard and respected their views) the children she interviewed said they were not listened to (i.e. no action followed from what they said). While some define listening as an attitude, a stance, others argue that it implies action. Listening thus has two aspects which affect the determination of rights issues. While children, like adults, have a right to be heard the factors that determine how that right is effected by adults who have responsibility for their care and safety are clear from these studies.

The studies reported thus strongly support the view that the promotion of children's participation in social work transactions depends upon the practitioners' skills in forging and maintaining a meaningful relationship. The relationship is built upon a combination of personal and professional qualities (they were kind, helpful and attentive) while at the same time they exercised professional skills (turning up on time, checking out the child's understanding, keeping them informed and offering a range of ways of participating). For these children there was no substitute for a fruitful relationship with their social worker. Their understanding and experience of being involved, represented or offered choice hinged more upon their experience of being attended to – of being listened to, heard and treated with care and respect – than on more mechanistic procedural strategies. The stance of the social worker thus needs to model an interaction that is supportive, companionable and constant.

In relation to meetings a number of aspects facilitated participation. A neutral venue was important. Information about the purpose, process and agenda needed to be provided beforehand, and opportunities made for negotiation to ensure the child's concerns were included. Also beforehand, issues of membership and confidentiality needed to be settled, and time given to discussing choices of participation – be they physical presence, advocacy, representation or written or audio material. Clear explanations about what might be possible or impossible were also essential if tokenism was to be avoided.

Before turning to the role of the agency and organisational culture in supporting best practice, I will briefly revisit the barriers illustrated by the studies. Coming first is the difficulty of balancing children's wishes and rights with what the adults responsible for their care consider to be key to the child's safety. Then comes the related aspect – the structures and procedures that are in place in social work organisations for facilitating children's participation. And third is current policy.

The ethics of care versus the ethics of rights

Gilligan (1982) helpfully distinguishes between a morality based purely on rights, which emphasises the independence and agency of an individual in decision making, and a morality based on the ethics of care, which emphasises people's interdependence and the context within which they make decisions. As has been clear throughout, these difficulties are fundamental to considering children's participation in social work decision making. And different views appertain as to how that balance should be achieved.

The research on children's involvement in child protection conferences and reviews highlighted a number of issues which are common to this debate. In complex situations of risk and abuse, social workers have to make caution and safety a priority. They have a responsibility of care, and may properly determine that the child will be damaged by hearing some of what is said in a meeting or reading some material written on a record. Their judgement may be to advise children not to attend a meeting or not to look at a record – to explain carefully why their wishes cannot be met and to discuss other ways they could communicate their views. While the studies reported here all describe children's feelings of being let down when what they want cannot be delivered, at the same time their safety must come first.

This point highlights another aspect of the tension between care matters and rights issues. In all the studies reported here, information sharing was problematic. Generally, the children were not in control of what information was shared or who it was shared with. Multi-agency meetings raised additional problems. In all the studies children felt unhappy about intimate family information being disclosed in a public arena. But in some cases, the children's wishes had to be over-ruled, and a balance struck taking into account the cost of losing the child's willingness to confide. Power imbalance is inherent – but must be managed, not avoided. A recognition that children also hold power and bring expertise may facilitate the management of this.

A scaffolding built for adults
Structures

A second factor that is key to children's participation in social work revolves around the structures within which social workers practise. Related to this are differing concepts of time. The studies reported here replicate findings from others, that the scaffolding of their encounters is constructed by adults, for adults. This was true of meetings and reviews, where young people seemed often reluctant to be involved and found them boring because they did not address their concerns. In the local authority survey some older children wanted to attend reviews, but felt they did not influence decisions. Equally, in the family group conferences, the location, the participants, the agenda, the structure and the plan were generally determined by the convener or the social worker – not by the child. While in some, the children did feel empowered by their opportunity to talk openly with their family about very personal matters, and some experienced their advocate as helpful, in others family groupings rendered open discussion unhelpful or disturbing and the social workers or the convener needed to exercise control.

Social work recording systems are also designed by adults, for adults. The Assessment Framework and the ICS recording systems currently being used are structured around the adult-determined process of assessment to review. They comprise a sequence of tick boxes and sections. In both the ICS study and the local authority survey, social workers said that the record systems did not elicit information from children, neither were they effective as tools for communicating with them. The ICS disability substudy raised a number of issues of the format and design of records which made the narrative hard to follow, with the likely effect of deterring young people from reading or contributing to them. It is hardly surprising that, as the ICS study found, many children take little interest in their records, portraying patterns of service delivery which do not encourage their participation, nor lead them to see the possible benefits of it.

The adult structuring of services also impacted at a wider level on the ways in which children's views on service provision were gained and fed back into local authority services. This point connects with the weight that is, or can appropriately be, given to children's views. All of the respondents in the local authority survey felt that young people's views were not accorded enough weight. The reasons given were either internal to the organisation (that the culture needed to change) or external (that the barriers were endemic to the professional role of balancing wishes with needs).

Time

Another factor influencing children's views about their involvement in social work processes was time. Children's time scales are different from adults. Taking a chronological approach to a process which makes sense to adults does not work in the same way for children. Children live in the present and do not have an adult conception of the future – so improvements in the present can be all important to them. They say 'but what about the future?' And they said we do not want to agonise over the past. If things have improved they may want to be left alone – so they disengage.

More commonly children's recall is of the feelings associated with an event – not with what actually happened. For what actually happened they are reliant on adults to explain in language which they understand. This brings us to the third and critical area which the research studies have highlighted: that it is the social worker's skills in communicating and in building trusting relationships that are fundamental to enabling children's meaningful involvement in decision making.

Current policy

As is apparent from the above discussion, in child and family social work the opportunities for and the reality of the child's participation in the transaction depend largely upon the way in which the social worker manages structures and relationships. In meetings the management style of the independent reviewing officer, chairperson or convener is also important. What enables the staff to set up and maintain participatory practices is the culture of the organisation.

In the local authority study a number of the managers ascribed the difficulty in responding to the children's views on service provision as being culture and ethos, with some seeing children's rights as a threat. This study demonstrated that progress in involving children in policy planning and delivery is slow and requires organisational change from senior management down to frontline staff. As Wright *et al.* (2006) suggest, a whole systems approach needs to be in place across the four levels of culture, structure, practice and effective review. And attention needs to be paid, in particular, to enabling children's inclusion in recording, and to setting up structures and procedures that are user friendly and enable them to participate in assessments, planning and in meetings.

In the ICS study the concern of both the managers and practitioners focused on the managerial culture underpinning the electronic recording system. Their concerns were two-fold: that the conception of good practice had become part of a culture where observance of procedures and targets was rated more highly than the individual skills of engagement and relationship building. And second, that the time available for direct work with children and families was drastically curtailed by the time spent in front of a computer. The recording system thus challenged the traditional role and values of social work sustained through positive personal engagement, as well as the time available to do it.

There are increasing concerns that the new information technologies, such as CAF and ICS (see White *et al.* 2009) focus on auditing and monitoring professional behaviour rather than facilitating practitioners' involvement in their work. The worry is that, since social workers are not currently involved in the way in which information technology is used they will be unable to influence the impact it has on service users and, in the words of Sapey (1997) 'further fail to control the ways in which computers affect the nature of social work itself' (p.803).

Research in Australia provides a similar account of the impact of office technologies on professional values. Reporting on two case studies in several Australian agencies, Burton and van den Broek (2009) conclude:

> The supposed efficiency and increased organisational accountability that resulted from the introduction of these technologies challenges the views of professionalism held… Increased emphasis on managerial and bureaucratic interest in accumulating data and reports refocused works priorities away from…client support to bureaucratic rather than professional accountabilities. (p.1339)

The last two decades have seen social work with children becoming increasingly enveloped by procedures with practitioners feeling besieged and demoralised, and their values of relationship and empathy getting lost in the discourse of targets and business management. The combined effect of the managerial culture alongside computer usage and standardised forms risks dehumanising and bringing rigidity to the relationship between child and social worker. And it can control discourses.

Appleton and Stanley (2008) describe some practitioners as 'feeling that they are drowning under a sea of bureaucracy, documentation and guidance' (p.1). Clearly organisations must support participatory practice by endorsing the values of human relationship and mirroring that in their modes of management. A consideration of how structures, for example, of meetings and reviews adversely affect the process could also lead to changing them, to making them more child friendly.

It is to be hoped that the Social Work Task Force (2009) set up by New Labour after the death of Peter Connelly to advise on training will bear fruit and promote optimism. The post qualification training of social workers in direct work with children is planned to improve through the reform of the children's workforce and through a number of training initiatives. And the flexibility now authorised to children's departments to modify the ICS recording system may result in user-friendly records to which children want to contribute.

Providing additional training in direct work with children and in participatory practice skills is important. What also needs to shift, from government level down, is the ethos and culture – from a culture where social work with children is now enveloped by procedures and heavily bureaucratised tools of practice, back to a tradition where the social work values based on relationship and critical thinking are mirrored by their managers and the directors of children's services.

I will end with a message from one of our research participants: from a 16-year-old boy with some learning disability to the director:

> 'I would like social workers to speak to you as if you were an adult – in words you can understand – and to take you seriously.'

Bibliography

Achard, D. (1993) *Children: Rights and Childhood.* London: Routledge.

Advisory Group on Citizenship (1998) *Final Report: Education for Citizenship and the Teaching of Democracy in Schools.(The Crick Report.)* London: QCA.

Aiers, A. and Kettle, J. (1998) *When Things Go Wrong.* London: NISW.

Ainsworth, M., Blehar, M., Waters, E. and Wall, S. (1978) *Patterns of Attachment: A Psychological Study of the Strange Situation.* Hillsdale, NJ: Lawrence Erlbaum Associates.

Alderson, P. (2008) *Young Children's Rights: Exploring Beliefs, Principles and Practice,* 2nd edition. London: Jessica Kingsley Publishers.

Aldgate, J., Jones, D., Rose, W. and Jeffrey, C. (2006) *The Developing World of the Child.* London: Jessica Kingsley Publishers.

Aldridge, J. and Becker, S. (2003) *Children Caring for Parents with Mental Illness: Perspectives of Young Carers, Parents and Professionals.* Bristol: Policy Press.

Appleton, J. and Stanley, N. (2008) 'Safeguarding children – everyone's responsibility.' *Child Abuse Review 17,* 2, 1–5.

Ariès, P. (1962) *Centuries of Childhood.* London: Jonathon Cape.

Arnstein, S. (1969) 'Eight rungs on the ladder of citizen participation.' *Journal of American Institute of Planners, 35,* 4, 216–224.

Arnstein, R. (1972) 'Power to the People: an assessment of the community action and model cities experience.' *Public Administration Review 32,* 377–389.

Atwood, M. (1989) *Cat's Eye.* London: Bloomsbury.

Aubrey, C. and Dahl, S. (2006) 'Children's voices: the views of vulnerable children on their service providers and the relevance of services they receive.' *British Journal of Social Work 36,* 1, 21–39.

Badham, B. and Davies, T. (2007) 'The Active Involvement of Young People.' In R. Harrison, C. Benjamin, S. Curran and R. Hunter (eds) *Leading Work with Young People.* Milton Keynes: OU and Sage.

Baldry, S. and Kemmis, J. (1996) *What it is to be Looked After by Camden. A report for Camden Social Services Department.* Camden: Camden Social Services Department.

Barford, R. (1993) *Children's Views of Child Protection Social Work.* Norwich: University of East Anglia.

Barnado's (2008) 'The shame of Britain's intolerance to children.' Press release, 17 November. Available at www.barnardos.org.uk/news_and_events/media_centre/press_releases/press_releases_archive.htm?ref=42088&year=2008&month=11, accessed on 20 June 2011.

Barnes, V. (2007) 'Young people's views of children's rights and advocacy services: a case for caring advocacy.' *Child Abuse Review 16,* 3, 140–153.

Barnes, V. and Davis, J. (2002) *Getting it Right for Children and Young People.* London: NCH.

Bell, C. (2011) Personal communication.

Bell, M. (1995) 'A study of the attitudes of nurses to the involvement of parents in the initial child protection conference, and their preparation for it.' *Journal of Advanced Nursing 22,* 250–257.

Bell, M. (1996a) 'An account of the experiences of 51 families involved in an initial child protection conference.' *Child and Family Social Work 1,* 43–55.

Bell, M. (1996b) 'Why some conferences are difficult: a study of the professionals' experience of some initial child protection conferences.' *Children and Society 10*, 51–63.

Bell, M. (1999a) 'The Looking After Children Materials: a critical analysis of their use in practice.' *Adoption and Fostering 22*, 4, 15–23.

Bell, M. (1999b) 'Working in partnership in child protection: the conflicts.' *The British Journal of Social Work 29*, 437–455.

Bell, M. (1999c) *Child Protection: Families and the Conference Process.* Aldershot: Ashgate.

Bell, M. (2000a) 'Domestic Violence and the Professional Response.' In U. McCluskey and C.A. Hooper (eds) *Psychodynamic Perspectives on Abuse: The Cost of Fear.* London: Jessica Kingsley Publishers.

Bell, M. (2000b) *Children Speak Out: An Exploration of the Views of Children and Young People Aged 8–16 of Their Experiences of a Child Protection Investigation.* York: University of York.

Bell, M. (2002) 'Promoting children's rights through the use of relationship.' *Child and Family Social Work 7*, 1, 1–11.

Bell, M. (2003) 'Working with Violent Families.' In M. Bell and K. Wilson (eds) *The Practitioners Guide to Working with Families.* Basingstoke: Palgrave.

Bell, M. (2004) 'Child protection at the community level.' *Child Abuse Review 13*, 6, 3–6.

Bell, M. (2007a) 'Community based parenting programmes: an exploration of the interplay between environmental and organisational factors in a Webster Stratton project.' *British Journal of Social Work 35*, 1–18.

Bell, M. (2007b) 'Case Conferences in Child Protection.' In K. Wilson and A. James (eds) *The Child Protection Handbook.* Edinburgh: Elsevier.

Bell, M., Crawshaw, M. and Wilson, K. (2001) *The Views of Approved Adopters on Their Preparation and Assessment for Adoption.* York: University of York.

Bell, M. and Fisher, T. (2004) *Family Foundations: An Evaluation of an Inter-agency Approach to Parenting under Stress – the Webster Stratton Parenting Programme.* York: Joseph Rowntree Foundation.

Bell, M., Shaw, I., Sinclair, I., Sloper, P. and Rafferty, J. (2007) *The Integrated Children's System: An Evaluation of the Practice, Process and Consequences of the ICS in CSSRs. Report to the Department for Education and Skills and WAG.* York: University of York.

Bell, M., Shaw, I., Sinclair, I., Sloper, P. *et al.* (2008) 'The Integrated Children's System – Is it fit for purpose?' *Community Care*, 21 April.

Bell, M. and Wilson, K. (2002) *A Report on Services in the Statutory and Voluntary Sector for Listening and Responding to Children and Young People in Kingston upon Hull.* York: University of York.

Bell, M. and Wilson, K. (2006) 'Children's views of family group conferences.' *British Journal of Social Work 36*, 1–11.

Bell, M., Wilson, K. and Crawshaw, M. (2002) 'Managing diversity in preparation for adoption.' *Adoption and Fostering 26*, 3, 8–19.

Bennett, R. (2008) 'Pressures of consumerism make children depressed.' *The Times*, 26 February.

Beresford, B. (1997) *Personal Accounts: Involving Disabled Children in Research.* London: HMSO.

Berridge, D. (1997) *Foster Care: A Research Review.* London: HMSO.

Bessell, S. (2009) 'Influencing international child labour policy: the potentials and limits of children-centred research.' *Children and Youth Services Review* (Special Issue).

Bilson, A. and White, S. (2005) 'Representing children's views and best interests in court: an international comparison.' *Child Abuse Review 14*, 4, 220–239.

Birmingham Safeguarding Children Board (2010) *Serious Case Review under Chapter VIII, 'Working Together to Safeguard Children': Case Number 14.* Available at www.lscbbirmingham. org.uk/downloads/Case+14.pdf, accessed on 13 July 2011.

Borland, M., Hill, M., Laybourne, A. and Stafford, A. (2001) *Improving Consultation with Children and Young People in Relevant Aspects of Policy Making and Legislation in Scotland.* Glasgow: Centre of the Child and Society, University of Glasgow and Children First.

Boseley, S. (2008) 'Poverty puts children at higher risk of accidents.' *The Guardian,* 10 December. Available at www.guardian.co.uk/society/2008/dec/10/ children?INTCMP=SRCH, accessed on 20 June 2011.

Bowlby, J. (1969) *Attachment and Loss, Vol. 1: Attachment.* London: Hogarth Press.

Bowlby, J. (1977) 'The making and breaking of affectional bonds.' *British Journal of Psychiatry 130,* 201–210.

Bowlby, J. (1988) *A Secure Base: Clinical Applications of Attachment Theory.* London: Routledge.

Bradshaw, J. (2006) 'How has the child poverty rate and composition changed?' Background Paper for the JRF Report *What Will it Take to End Child Poverty in the UK?* York: University of York.

Bradshaw, J. and Mayhew, E. (eds) (2005) *The Wellbeing of Children in the UK.* London: Save the Children.

Brandon, M., Belderson, P., Warren, C., Howe, D. *et al.* (2008) *Analysing Child Deaths and Serious Injury Through Abuse and Neglect: What Can We Learn?* London: DCSF.

Braye, S. (2000) 'Participation and Involvement in Social Care – An Overview.' In H. Kemshall and R. Littlechild (eds) *User Involvement and Participation in Social Care.* London: Jessica Kingsley Publishers.

Braye, S. and Preston-Shoot, M. (1995) *Empowering Practice in Social Care.* Buckingham: Open University Press.

Brayne, H. and Carr, H. (2008) *Law for Social Workers,* 10th edition. Oxford: Oxford University Press.

Bristol City Council (2009) *The Pledge to Children in Care and Care Leavers.* Available at www. bristol-cyps.org.uk/policies/pdf/cic-bristol-pledge.pdf, accessed on 20 June 2011.

Broad, B. (1998) *Young People Leaving Care.* London: Jessica Kingsley Publishers.

Bronfenbrenner, U. (1979) *The Ecology of Human Development.* Cambridge, Mass: Harvard University Press.

Brown, L. (2003) 'Mainstream or margin? The current use of family group conferences in child welfare practice in the UK.' *Child and Family Social Work 8,* 331–340.

Burton, J. and van den Broek, P. (2009) 'Accountable and countable: information systems and the bureacratisation of social work.' *British Journal of Social Work 39,* 7, 1326–1342.

Butler, I., Scanlon, L., Robinson, M., Douglas, G. and Murch, M. (2002) 'Children's involvement in their parents' divorce: implications for practice.' *Children and Society 16,* 89–102.

Butler, I. and Williamson, H. (1994) *Children Speak: Trauma and Social Work.* Harlow: Longman.

Cairns, L. (2001) 'Investing in children: learning how to promote the rights of all children.' *Children and Society 15,* 5, 347–360.

Cairns, L. and Brannen, M. (2005) 'Promoting the human rights of children and young people: the "Investing in Children" experience.' *Adoption and Fostering 29,* 1, 78–87.

Calder, M. and Horwarth, J. (1999) *Working for Children on the Child Protection Register.* Aldershot: Ashgate.

Calam, R.M., Cox, A.D., Glasgow, D.V. *et al.* (2005) *In My Shoes: A Computer Assisted Interview for Communicating with Children and Vulnerable Adults.* University of Manchester. Available at www.inmyshoes.org.uk/In_My_Shoes/About, accessed on 20 June 2011.

Carr, S. (2004) *Has Service-user Participation Made a Difference to Social Care Services?* London: Social Care Institute for Excellence.

Carroll, J. (2002) 'Play therapy: the children's views.' *Child and Family Social Work* 7, 177–187.

Chand, A. (2005) 'Do you speak English? Language barriers in child protection social work with minority ethnic families.' *British Journal of Social Work* 6, 801–821.

Children Act (1989) London: HMSO.

Children Act (2004) London: HMSO.

Children in Care Councils Consortium First Report (2009), London: National Children's Bureau.

Children and Young People's Unit (2001) *Learning to Listen: Core Principles for the Involvement of Children and Young People.* London: Children and Young People's Unit.

Children's Commissioner for Wales (2009) *Children's Commissioner for Wales: Annual Review 07–08.* Swansea: Children's Commissioner for Wales. Available at www.childcom.org.uk/uploads/publications/18.pdf, accessed on 20 June 2011.

Children's Society (2006) *The Good Childhood? A Question for our Times.* London: The Children's Society.

Children's Society (2009) *The Good Childhood: Searching for Values in a Competitive Age.* London: The Children's Society.

Chong, H. (2006) *'The Experiences and Needs of Children of Chinese Origin in England: The Family, Schools and Child Support Services.'* Unpublished PhD thesis, University of York.

Christensen, P. and James, A. (2000) *Research with Children.* London: Falmouth Press.

Clark, A. (2004) 'The Mosaic Approach and Research with Young Children.' In V. Lewis, C. Kellett, S. Robinson, D. Fraser and S. Ding (eds) *The Reality of Research with Children and Young People.* London: Sage.

Clark, A. and Moss, P. (2001) *Listening to Young Children. The Mosaic Approach.* London: National Children's Bureau Enterprises and Joseph Rowntree Foundation.

Cleaver, H. and Walker, S. with Meadows, P. (2004) *Assessing Children's Needs and Circumstances.* London: Jessica Kingsley Publishers.

Cleaver, H., Walker, S., Scott, J., Cleaver, D. *et al.* (2008) *The Integrated Children's System.* London: Jessica Kingsley Publishers.

Cleveland Report (1988) *Report of the Inquiry into Child Abuse in Cleveland.* London: HMSO.

Coetzee, J.M. (1997) *Boyhood: Scenes from Provincial Life.* London: Virago.

Compass Report (2006) 'Commercialisation of childhood.' Available at www.compassonline.org.uk/campaigns/campaign.asp?n=446, accessed on 10 May 2010.

Connexions (2001) *The Active Involvement of Young People in the Connexions Service.* London: Department for Education and Skills.

Connolly, P. (2005) 'Children, assessment and computer-assisted interviewing.' *Child Abuse Review 14*, 6, 407–414.

Coombe, V. (2002) *Up for It: Getting Young People Involved in Local Government.* Leicester: National Youth Agency

Corden, J. and Preston-Shoot, M. (1987) *Contracts in Social Work.* Aldershot: Gower.

Crow, G. and Marsh, P. (2000) *Family Group Conferences in Youth Justice.* Family and Welfare Findings Series 6. Sheffield: University of Sheffield.

Cuthbert, C. and Hatch, R. (2008) *Educational Aspiration and Attainment amongst Young People in Deprived Communities.* Bristol: Policy Press.

Cutler, D. (2003) *Organisational Standards and Young People's Participation in Public Decision Making.* London: Carnegie Young People Initiative.

Dally, J. (2006) 'Contact or No Contact after Adoption: What it Means and How it Affects Family Life, Attachment and Identity.' Unpublished PhD thesis, University of York.

Dalrymple, J. (2002) 'Family group conferences and youth advocacy: the participation of children and young people in family decision making.' European Journal of Social Work 5, 3, 287–299.

Dalrymple, J. (2005) 'Constructions of child and youth advocacy: emerging issues in advocacy practice.' Children and Society 19, 3–15.

Daniel, G. (2008) 'Talking with Children.' In P. Kennison and A. Goodman (eds) Children as Victims. Exeter: Learning Matters.

Danso, C., Greaves, H., Howell, S., Ryan, M., Sinclair, R. and Tunnard, J. (2003) The Involvement of Children and Young People in Promoting Change and Enhancing the Quality of Social Care. London: National Children's Bureau.

Darbyshire, P. (2000) 'Guest editorial: from research on children to research with children.' Neonatal, Paediatric and Child Health Nursing 3, 1, 2–3.

Darbyshire, P., MacDougall, C. and Schiller, W. (2005) 'Multiple methods in qualitative research with children: more insight or just more?' Qualitative Research 5, 4, 417–436.

Davey, C. (2010) Children's Participation in Decision-Making: A Summary Report on Progress. London: CRAE and NCB.

Davey, C., Burke, T. and Shaw, C. (2010) Children's Participation in Decision-making: A Children's Views Report. Available at www.participationworks.org.uk/npf/publications. Accessed on 12 October 2010.

Davies, M. and Morgan, A. (2005) 'Using computer-assisted interviewing (CASI) questionnaires to facilitate consultation and participation with vulnerable young people.' Child Abuse Review 14, 389–406.

De Boer, C. and Coady, N. (2007) 'Good helping relationships in child welfare: learning from stories of success.' Child and Family Social Work 12, 32–42.

Denzin, N. (1977) Childhood Socialization. San Francisco: Jossey-Bass.

Department for Children, Schools and Families (DCSF) (2006) Care Matters: Transforming the Lives of Children and Young People in Care. London: DCSF.

Department for Children, Schools and Families (2007a) Children and Young People Today. London: HMSO.

Department for Children, Schools and Families (2007b) The Children's Plan: Building Brighter Futures. London: HMSO.

Department for Children, Schools and Families (2007c) Aiming High for Young People. London: HMSO.

Department for Children, Schools and Families (2008a) Working Together: Listening to the Voices of Children and Young People. London: DCSF.

Department for Children, Schools and Families (2008b) Care Matters: Time to Deliver for Children in Care. London: DCSF.

Department for Children, Schools and Families (2009a) Integrated Children's System: ICS Guidance Note: The ICS and Inoperability. London: DCSF.

Department for Children, Schools and Families (2009b) Letter from Baroness Morgan to DCSs. London: DCSF.

Department for Children, Schools and Families (2010) Working Together to Safeguard Children: A Guide to Inter-Agency Working to Safeguard and Promote the Welfare of Children. London: DCSF.

Department for Education and Employment (1998) Education for Citizenship and the Teaching of Democracy in Schools. Qualifications and Curriculum Authority. London: HMSO.

Department for Education and Skills (DfES) (2003a) *Get It Sorted: Providing Effective Advocacy Services for Children and Young People.* London: HMSO.

Department for Education and Skills (2003b) *Every Child Matters.* Cmnd 5806. London: TSO.

Department for Education and Skills (2004a) *Every Child Matters.* London: HMSO.

Department for Education and Skills (2004b) *Every Child Matters: Next Steps.* London: HMSO.

Department for Education and Skills (2004c) *Working Together: Giving Children and Young People a Say.* London: HMSO.

Department for Education and Skills (2005a) *Youth Matters*, Cm 6629. London: HMSO.

Department for Education and Skills (2005b) *Integrated Children's System: A Statement of Business Requirements.* London: DfES.

Department for Education and Skills (2006) *Care Matters: Transforming the Lives of Children and Young People in Care.* London: DfES.

Department for Education and Skills (2007) *Care Matters: Consultation Response.* London: TSO.

Department of Environment, Transport and the Regions (1998) *Modernising Local Government.* London: TSO.

Department of Health (1991) *Working Together Under the Children Act.* London: HMSO.

Department of Health (1995) *The Challenge of Partnership in Child Protection: Practice Guide.* London: HMSO.

Department of Health (1998) *Social Services Facing the Future. The Seventh Annual Report of the Chief Inspector.* Social Services Inspectorate. London: Department of Health.

Department of Health (1999) *Working Together to Safeguard Children: A Guide to Inter Agency Working to Safeguard and Promote the Welfare of the Child.* London: HMSO.

Department of Health (2000) *Framework for the Assessment of Children in Need and Their Families.* London: HMSO.

Department of Health (2001) *The Quality Protects Programme: Transforming Children's Services.* London: HMSO.

Department of Health (2002a) *National Standards for Agencies Providing Advocacy for Children and Young People in England.* London: HMSO.

Department of Health (2002b) *National Minimum Standards for Children in Care.* London: Department of Health.

Department of Health (2003) *Getting the Right Start: National Service Framework for Children – Emerging Findings.* London: HMSO.

Department of Health (2004) *National Service Framework for Children, Young People and Maternity Services.* London: Department of Health.

Digital Exclusion Task Force (2009) *Digital Exclusion.* London: HMSO. Available at www.publications.parliament.uk/pa/cm200910/cmselect/cmbis/72/7209.htm, accessed on 20 June 2011.

Dixon, J. (2008) 'Young people leaving care: health, well-being and outcomes.' *Child and Family Social Work 13*, 207–217.

Dobrowski, S., Gishlar, K. and Durst, T. (2007) 'Safeguarding young people from cyber pornography and cyber sexual predation: a major dilemma of the internet.' *Child Abuse Review 16*, 153–170.

Edleson, H. (1999) 'Children witnessing adult domestic violence.' *Journal of Interpersonal Violence 14*, 839–870.

Education Act (2002) London: HMSO.

Education and Skills Select Committee (2007) 'Inquiry into citizenship education.' Available at www. Select-committee-inquiry-into-citizenship-education. Accessed on 10 May 2011.

Egelund, T. (2006) 'Bureaucracy or professionalism? The work tools of child protection services.' *Scandinavian Journal of Social Welfare 5*, 165–174.

Erikson, E. (1968) *Identity, Youth and Crisis*. London: Faber and Faber.

Evans, P. and Fuller, M. (2006) 'Hello. Who am I speaking to? Communicating with pre-school children in educational research settings.' *Early Years 17*, 1, 17–20.

Family Rights Group (2008) *Using Family Group Conferences for Children who are or may become Subject to Public Law Proceedings*. London: FRG.

Featherstone, B. (2004) 'Family life and family support: a feminist perspective.' *British Journal of Social Work 35*, 8, 1343–1351.

Ferguson, H. (2009) 'Performing child protection: home visiting, movement and the struggle to reach the abused child.' *Child and Family Social Work 14*, 4, 471–480.

Fox Harding, L. (1991) *Perspectives in Child Care Policy*. Harlow: Longman.

Franklin, B. (ed.) (2001) *The New Handbook of Children's Rights: Comparative Policy and Practice*. London: Routledge.

Franklin, A. and Sloper, P. (2004) 'Participation of Disabled Children in Decision Making in Social Services Departments in England.' *Cash and Care: The Newsletter of the SPRU*. York: University of York.

Franklin, A. and Sloper, P. (2006) 'Participation of disabled children and young people in decision making within social service departments: a survey of current and recent activities in England.' *British Journal of Social Work 36*, 5, 723–741.

Franklin, A. and Sloper, P. (2009) 'Supporting the participation of disabled children and young people in decision making.' *Children and Society 23*, 1, 3–15.

Freud, S. (1923) 'The Ego and the Id.' In J. Strachey (ed.) *The Standard Edition of the Psychological Works of Sigmund Freud*. (Vol.19) London: Hogarth.

Frost, N. (2002) *RHP Companion to Family Support*. London: Russell House.

Frost, N. and Featherstone, B. (2003) 'Families, Social Change and Diversity.' In M. Bell, M. and K. Wilson (eds) *The Practitioner's Guide to Working with Families*. Basingstoke: Palgrave.

Fry, E. (2003) *Listen Then Commission*. London: Who Cares? Trust and The Fostering Network.

Gallagher, B. (2005) 'New technology: helping or harming children.' *Child Abuse Review 14*, 6, 367.

Garboden, M. (2010) 'Facing up to obstructive parents.' *Community Care*, 10 August.

Garrett, P. (2005) 'Social work's electronic turn: notes on the deployment of information and communication technologies in social work with children and families.' *Critical Social Policy 25*, 4, 529.

Garrett, P. (2007) 'Making "anti-social behaviour": a fragment in the evolution of ASBO politics in Britain.' *British Journal of Social Work 37*, 5, 839–856.

Giddens, A. (1991) *Modernity and Self-Identity: Self and Society in the Late Modern Age*. Cambridge: Polity Press.

Gilbert, R., Spatz Widom, C., Browne, K., Fergusson, D., Webb, E. and Janson, S. (2008) 'Child Maltreatment 1: Burden and consequences of child maltreatment in high-income countries.' *The Lancet*, 3 December.

Gillick v West Norfolk and Wisbech Area Health Authority and Another (1986) AC.112.

Gilligan, C. (1982) *In a Different Voice*. Cambridge, Mass: Harvard University Press.

Gilligan, R. (2001) *Promoting Resilience: A Resource Guide on Working with Children in the Care System*. London: BAAF.

Golding, W. (1954) *Lord of the Flies*. London: Faber and Faber.

Goldsmith, L. (1999) *Recording with care: inspection of case recording in social services departments*. London: Social Services Inspectorate. Available at http://webarchive. nationalarchives.gov.uk/+/www.dh.gov.uk/en/Publicationsandstatistics/Publications/ PublicationsPolicyAndGuidance/DH_4010129, accessed on 20 June 2011.

Goldson, B. (2000) *Parenting Orders and Policy Developments in Youth Justice*. London: Sage.

Grimshaw, R. and McGuire, C. (1998) *Evaluating Parenting Programmes: A Study of Stakeholders' Views*. York: Joseph Rowntree Foundation.

Grimshaw, R. and Sinclair, R. (1997) *Planning to Care: Regulation, Procedure and Practice under the Children Act 1*. London: National Children's Bureau.

Hallett, C. and Prout, A. (2003) *Hearing the Voices of Children: Social Policy for a New Century*. London: Routledge-Falmer.

Hart, R. (1992) *Children's Participation: From Tokenism to Citizenship*. London: UNICEF International Child Development Centre.

Hart, R. (1997) *Children's Participation: The Theory and Practice of Involving Young Citizens in Community Development and Environmental Care*. New York: UNICEF.

Hart, S., Price Cohen, C., Farrell Erickson, M. and Flekkøy, M.G. (eds) (2001) *Children's Rights in Education*. London: Jessica Kingsley Publishers.

Head, A. (1998) 'The child's voice in child and family social work decision making: the perspective of the guardian ad litem.' *Child and Family Social Work 3*, 89–196.

Hemmings, P., Smith, S. C. and Pennells, M. (eds) (1995) *Communicating with Children Through Play: Interventions with Bereaved Children*. London: Jessica Kingsley Publishers.

Hendrick, H. (1997) *Children, Childhood and English Society, 1880–1990*. Cambridge: Cambridge University Press.

Hester, M., Pearson, C. and Harwin, N. (2007) *Making an Impact: Children and Domestic Violence: A Reader*. London: Jessica Kingsley Publishers.

Hill, M. (1997) 'Ethical Issues in Qualitative Methodology with Children.' In D. Hogan and R. Gilligan (eds) *Researching Children's Experiences: Qualitative Approaches*. Dublin: The Children's Research Centre, Trinity College.

Hill, M. (2006) 'Children's voices on ways of having a voice: children and young people perspectives on methods used in research and consultation.' *Childhood 13*, 1, 69–89.

Hill, M., Davies, J., Prout, A. and Tisdall, K. (2004) 'Moving the participation agenda forward.' *Children and Society 18*, 2, 77–96.

HM Government (2006) *Working Together to Safeguard Children: A Guide to Inter-agency Working to Safeguard and Promote the Welfare of Children*. London: TSO.

HM Treasury (2007) *Aiming High for Children: Supporting Families*. London: HMSO.

Hobbes, T. (1660) *The Leviathan*. Cambridge & New York: Cambridge University Press.

Hobcroft, J. (2007) 'Child development, the life course and social exclusion: are the frameworks used in the UK relevant for developing countries?' *Chronic Poverty Research Centre, Working Paper 72*, University of Manchester.

Hogan, D. (1997) 'Valuing the Child in Research: Historical and Current Influences on Research Methodology with Children.' In D. Hogan and R. Gilligan (eds) *Researching Children's Experiences: Qualitative Approaches*. Dublin: The Children's Research Centre, Trinity College Dublin.

Holland, S. (2006) 'We had to be there to make sure it was what we wanted.' *Childhood 13*, 1, 91–111.

Holland, S. (2010) 'Looked after children and the ethic of care.' *British Journal of Social Work 40*, 1664–1680.

House of Commons (2010) *United Kingdom Youth Parliament Debate*, 29 October. Available at www.ukyouthparliament.org.uk/downloads/UKYP_HCD_291010.pdf, accessed on 20 June 2011..

Howe, D. (1995) *Attachment Theory for Social Work Practice.* Basingstoke: Macmillan

Hutchby, I. and Moran-Ellis, J. (eds) (2001) *Children, Technology and Culture: The Impact of Technologies in Children's Everyday Lives.* London: Routledge.

Hutton, A. (2004) *What Works in Children and Young People's Participation.* Ilford: Barnardo's.

Institute for Public Policy Research (2002) *Involving Young People in Local Authority Decision Making.* York: Joseph Rowntree Foundation.

Jack, G. (2001) 'Ecological Perspectives in Assessing Children and Families.' In J. Horwath (ed.) *The Child's World: Assessing Children in Need.* London: Jessica Kingsley Publishers.

Jack, G. and Gil, O. (2010) 'The role of communities in safeguarding children and young people.' *Child Abuse Review* 19, 82–96.

Jackson, S. and Morris, K. (1999) 'Family group conferences: user empowerment or family self-reliance? A development from Lupton.' *British Journal of Social Work 29*, 621–630.

Jäger, J. (2009) *'An Introduction to Play Therapy.'* Unpublished thesis. York: University of York.

Jäger, J. and Ryan, V. (2007) 'Evaluating clinical practice: using play based techniques.' *Clinical Child Psychology and Psychiatry 12*, 3, 437–450.

James, A. and James, A. (2004) *Constructing Childhood: Theory, Policy and Social Practice.* Basingstoke: Palgrave.

James, A. and Prout, A. (1990) *Constructing and Reconstructing Childhood: Contemporary Issues in the Sociology of Childhood.* Basingstoke: Falmer Press.

John, M. (1996a) *Children in Charge: The Child's Right to a Fair Hearing.* London: Jessica Kingsley Publishers.

John, M. (1996b) *Children in Our Charge: The Child's Right to Resources.* London: Jessica Kingsley Publishers.

John, J. (1996c) *A Charge Against Society: Children's right to Protection.* London: Jessica Kingsley Publishers.

Jones, A. and Price, E. (2001) 'Bubbled Dialogue: Using Computer Application to Investigate Social Information Processing in Children with Emotional Difficulties.' In I. Hutchby and J. Moran Ellis (eds) *Children, Technology and Culture: The Impact of Technologies in Children's Everyday Lives.* London: Routledge.

Joyce, J. (1916) *A Portrait of the Artist as a Young Man.* New York: B.W. Huebsch.

Kakabadse, K., Kakabadse, N., Bailey, S. and Myers, A. (2009) *Techno Addicts: Young Person Addiction to Technology.* Cambridge: Sigel Press.

Katz, I. (1995) 'Approaches to Empowerment in Child Protection.' In C. Cloke and M. Davies (eds) *Participation and Empowerment in Child Protection.* London: Pitman.

Key, E. (1900) *The Century of the Child.* Stockholm & New York: Arno Press.

Keys, S. (2009) 'Skills for child protection practice.' *Child Abuse Review 18*, 316–332.

Kiddle, C. (1999) *Traveller Children: A Voice for Themselves.* London: Jessica Kingsley Publishers.

Kirby, P., Lanyon, C., Cronin, K. and Sinclair, R. (2003) *Building a Culture of Participation: Involving Children and Young People in Policy, Service Planning, Delivery and Evaluation.* Research Report. London: Department for Education and Skills.

Kohli, R. (2006) 'The sound of silence: listening to what unaccompanied asylum-seeking children say and do not say.' *British Journal of Social Work 36*, 5, 707–722.

LAC (2000) *22: Quality Protects Programme: Transforming Children's Services 2001–2002.* London: DOH.

Laming, Lord (2003) *The Victoria Climbié Inquiry. Report of an Inquiry by Lord Laming.* Cmd 5730. London: HMSO.

Laming, Lord (2009) *The Protection of Children in England: A Progress Report.* London: DCSF.

Lansdown, G. (1995) *Taking Part: Children's Participation in Decision Making.* London: Institute of Policy Research.

Layard, R. (2009) *A Good Childhood: Searching for Values in a Competitive Age.* London: Penguin.

Lee, N. (2001) *Childhood and Society.* Buckingham: Open University Press.

Liebel, M. (2003) 'Working children as social subjects: the contribution of working children's organisations to social transformation.' *Childhood 10,* 3, 265–285.

Lightfoot, J. and Sloper, P. (2003) 'Having a say in health: guidelines for involving children and young people with a chronic or physical disability in local health services development.' *Children and Society 17,* 277–290.

Lister, R. (2005) 'Children and Citizenship.' Paper presented at Glasgow Centre for the Child and Society Seminar, 3 November.

Locke, J. (1960) 'An Essay concerning Human Understanding.' In J. L. Axtell (ed.) *The Educational Writings of John Locke.* Cambridge: Cambridge University Press. [Essay originally published in 1693.]

Lonne, B., Parton, N., Thompson, J. and Harries, M. (2008) *Reforming Child Protection.* Oxford: Routledge.

Lupton, C. and Nixon, P. (1999) *Empowering Practice: A Critical Appraisal of the Family Group Conference Approach.* Bristol: Policy Press.

Lupton, C. and Stevens, M. (1997) *Family Outcomes: Following through on Family Group Conferences.* SSRIU report No 34. Portsmouth: University of Portsmouth.

Lyon, C. and Parton, N. (1995) 'Children's Rights and the Children Act 1989.' In B. Franklin *The Handbook of Children Rights.* London: Routledge.

McCourt, F. (1996) *Angela's Ashes.* New York: Scribner.

McLeod, A. (2008) *Listening to Children: A Practitioner's Guide.* London: Jessica Kingsley Publishers.

McLeod, A. (2010) 'A friend and equal: do young people in care seek the impossible from their social workers?' *British Journal of Social Work 40,* 3, 772–788.

McNeish, D., Newman, T. and Roberts, H. (2002) *What Works for Children.* Philadelphia: Open University Press.

Main, M. and Solomon, J. (1986) *Discovery of an Insecure-disorganised/Disorientated Attachment Pattern: Affective Development in Infancy.* Norwood, NJ: Ablex.

Mars, M. (1989) 'Child Sexual Abuse and Race Issues.' In British Association for Adoption and Fostering (ed.) *After Abuse Papers: Papers on Caring and Planning for a Child Who Has Been Sexually Abused.* London: BAAF.

Marsh, P. and Crow, G. (1998) *Family Group Conferences in Child Welfare.* Oxford: Blackwell Science.

Marsh, P. and Fisher, M. (1992) *Good Intentions: Developing Partnership in Social Services.* York: Joseph Rowntree Foundation.

May, C. (2002) *The Information Society.* Cambridge: Polity Press.

Mayall, B. (2002) *Towards a Sociology for Childhood: Thinking from Children's Lives.* Maidenhead: Open University Press.

Merkel-Holguin, L., Nixon, P. and Burford, G. (2003) 'Learning with families: a synopsis of FGDM research and evaluation in child welfare.' *Protecting Children 18,* 1–12.

Middleton, E. (2006) 'Youth participation in the UK: bureaucratic disaster or triumph of child rights.' *Children, Youth and Environments 16,* 2.

Mitchell, W., Franklin, A., Greco, V. and Bell, M. (2009) 'Working with children with learning disabilities and/or who communicate non-verbally: research experiences and their implications for social work education.' *Social Work Education Journal 28*, 3, 309–317.

Mitchell, W. and Sloper, P. (2009) 'The Integrated Children's System and disabled children.' *Child and Family Social Work 13*, 274–285.

Morris, J. (1999) *Space for Us: Finding Out What Disabled Children and Young People Think About Their Placements.* London: London Borough of Newham.

Morris, J. (2003) 'Including all children: finding out about the experiences of children with communication and/or cognitive impairments.' *Children and Society 17*, 337–348.

Morrow, V. (2001) 'Using qualitative methods to elicit young people's perspectives on their environments: some ideas for community health initiatives.' *Health Education Research 16*, 3, 155–168.

Morrow, V. and Richards, M. (1996) 'The ethics of social research with children: an overview.' *Children and Society 10*, 90–105.

Moss, P. (2001) 'Where next for childcare.' *Childcare Now 13*, 1–4.

Moss, P. (2002) 'From Children's Services to Children's Spaces.' Paper presented at Seminar 1, ESRC series, Challenging Social Inclusion, University of Edinburgh.

Mullender, A., Hague, G., Imam, U., Kelly, L., Malos, E. and Regan, L. (2002) *Children's Perspectives on Domestic Violence.* London: Sage.

Munro, E. (2001) 'Empowering looked after children.' *Child and Family Social Work 6*, 2, 129–137.

Munro, E. (2005) 'What tools do we need to improve identification of child abuse.' *Child Abuse Review 14*, 6, 374–388.

Munro, E. (2010) *The Munro Report on Child Protection.* Available at www.education.gov.uk/munroreview. Accessed 1 November 2010.

Murray, C. (2003) 'Children and young people's participation and non-participation in research.' *Adoption and Fostering 29*, 1, 57–66.

National Children's Bureau (2005) *My Turn to Talk.* London: NCB.

National Youth Advocacy Service (2009) *Making Choices.* London: NYAS.

National Youth Agency (2008) *Youth Participation Works In Youth Opportunity & Youth Capital Funding.* Available at www.participationworks.org.uk. Accessed 23 March 2011.

National Youth Agency (2009) *Young People's Participation in Children's Trusts.* Available at www.nya.org.uk/policy/research. Accessed on 18 April 2011.

Nelson, S. and Baldwin, N. (2002) 'Comprehensive neighbourhood mapping: developing a powerful tool for child protection.' *Child Abuse Review 11*, 4, 214–229.

Nixon, P., Burford, G. and Quinn, A. (2005) *A Survey of International Practices, Policy and Research on Family Group Conferences and Related Practices.* American Humane Association. Available at www.frg.org.uk/pdfs/Family%20Group%20practices%20report.pdf, accessed on 20 June 2011.

Nolan, M., Hanson, E., Grant, G., Keady, J. and Magnusson, L. (2007) 'Introduction: What Counts as Knowledge, Whose Knowledge Counts? Towards an Authentic Participatory Enquiry.' In M. Nolan, E. Hanson, G. Grant, J. Keady (eds) *User Participation in Health and Social Care Research.* Maidenhead: Open University Press.

NSPCC (2003) *It Doesn't Happen to Disabled Children. Child Protection and Disability.* London: NSPCC.

NSPCC (2007) *Your Shout Too! A Survey of the Views of Children and Young People Involved in Private Law Court Proceedings.* London: NSPCC.

NSPCC and Chailey Heritage (1996) *Turning Points: A Resource Pack for Communicating with Children.* Leicester: NSPCC and DOH.

O'Kane, C. (2009) 'The Development of Participatory Techniques: Facilitating Children's Views About Decisions that Affect them.' In P. Christensen and A. James (eds) *Research with Children*. London: Faber.

O'Kane, T. (2002) 'The Development of Participatory Techniques for Facilitating Children's Views About Decisions which Affect them.' In P. Christenson and A. James (eds) *Research with Children*. London: Falmer.

Ofsted (2003) *Bullying: Effective Action in Secondary Schools*. London: Ofsted.

Ofsted (2008) *Children's Views on Advocacy*. London: Ofsted.

Oldfield, C. and Fowler, C. (2004) *Mapping Children and Young People's Participation in England*. Nottingham: Department for Education and Skills.

Oliver, C., Knight, A. and Candappa, M. (2006) *Advocacy for Looked After Children and Children in Need: Achievements and Challenges*. London: Thomas Coram Research Unit, Institute of Education, University of London.

Park, A., Phillips, M. and Johnson, M. (2004) *Young People in Britain: The Attitudes and Experiences of 12–19 Year Olds*. London: Department for Education and Skills.

Parry, O., Pithouse, A., Anglim, C. and Batchelor, C. (2008) 'The tip of the iceberg: children's complaints and advocacy in Wales – an insider view from complaints officers.' *British Journal of Social Work 38*, 1, 5–19.

Parton, N. (1998) 'Risk, advanced liberalism and child welfare: the need to discover uncertainty and ambiguity.' *British Journal of Social Work 28*, 1, 5–28.

Parton, N. (2006) *Safeguarding Childhoods*. Basingstoke: Palgrave.

Pennell, J. and Burford, G. (2000) 'Family decision making and protecting children and women.' *Child Welfare 79*, 2, 131–158

Percy-Smith, B. (2009) *Evaluating the Development of Young People's Participation in Two Children's Trusts*. Bristol: The SOLAR Action Research Centre, University of the West of England.

Piaget, J. (1950) *The Psychology of Intelligence*. London: Routledge.

Piaget, J. (1959) *The Language and Thought of the Child*. London: Routledge and Keegan Paul.

Priestley, M. (2000) 'Adults only: disability, social policy and the life course.' *Journal of Social Policy 29*, 3, 421–439.

Prout, A. (2000) 'Children's participation: control and self realisation in British late modernity.' *Children and Society 15*, 3, 193–201.

Prout, A. (2002) 'Researching children as social actors: an introduction to the children 5–16 programme.' *Children and Society 16*, 67–76.

Rafferty, S. (2006) 'Giving children a voice? What next? A study from one primary school.' SCRE, *Spotlights 65*.

RE M (Abduction: child's objections) (2007) EWCA Civ 260. Court of Appeal. Available at www.dawsoncornwell.com/en/documents/20072FLR72.pdf, accessed on 20 June 2011.

Robbins, D. (2000) *Tracking Progress in Children's Services: An Evaluation of LA Responses to the Quality Protects Programme*. Year 2. National Overview Report. London: Department of Health.

Robbins, D. (2001) *Transforming Children's Services: An Evaluation of Local Responses to Quality Protects Programme*. Year 3. London: Department of Health.

Rousseau, J.J. (1991) *Emile or On Education*. Translated with introduction and notes by Allan Bloom. London: Penguin Classics.

Roy, A. (1997) *The God of Small Things*. London: Harper Perennial.

Rutter, M. (1972) *Maternal Deprivation Reassessed*. Harmondsworth: Penguin. (Reprinted 1981.)

Ryan, V., Wilson, K. and Fisher, T. (1995) 'Developing partnerships in therapeutic work with children.' *Journal of Social Work Practice 9*, 2, 131–140.

Ryburn, M. and Atherton, C. (1996) 'Family group conferences in practice.' *Adoption and Fostering 20*, 16–23.

Salmon, G. (2000) *E-Moderating: The Key to Teaching and Learning Online.* London: Kogan Page.

Sandbaek, S. (1999) 'Children with problems: focusing on everyday life.' *Children and Society 13*, 2, 106–118.

Sanders, R. and Mace, S. (2006) 'Agency policy and the participation of children and young people in the child protection process.' *Child Abuse Review 15*, 89–109.

Sapey, B. (1997) 'Social work tomorrow: towards a critical understanding of technology in social work.' *British Journal of Social Work 27*, 6, 803–814.

Schofield, G. (2005) 'The voice of the child in family placement making: a developmental model.' *Adoption and Fostering 29*, 1, 29–44.

Schofield, G. and Thoburn, J. (1996) *The Voice of the Child: Participation in Decision-making in Child Protection.* London: Institute for Public Policy Research.

Schorr, L. (1991) *Within Our Reach: Breaking the Circle of Disadvantage.* New York: Anchor Press.

Scutt, N. (1998) 'Child Advocacy.' In C. Cloke and M. Davis (eds) *Participation and Empowerment in Child Protection.* London: Pitman.

Shaw, I., Bell, M., Sinclair, I., Sloper, P., Rafferty, J. and Mitchell, W. (2009) 'An exemplary scheme? An evaluation of the Integrated Children's System.' *British Journal of Social Work 39*, 4, 613–626.

Shemmings, D. (1996) *Involving Children in Child Protection Conferences.* Social Work Monograph. Norwich: University of East Anglia.

Shemmings, D. (2000) 'Professional attitudes to children's participation in decision-making: dichotomous accounts and doctrinal contests.' *Child and Family Social Work 5*, 235–243.

Sheppard, A.M. (1994) *Ensuring Children's Voices are Heard in the Child Protection Process and Child Care Decision Making in Family Support Services.* London: Department of Health.

Shier, H. (2001) 'Pathways to participation: openings, opportunities and obligations.' *Children and Society 15*, 2, 107–117.

Sinclair, I., Wilson, K. and Gibbs, I. (2001) 'A life more ordinary: what children want from foster placements.' *Adoption and Fostering 25*, 4, 17–26.

Sinclair, I., Wilson, K. and Gibbs, I. (2004) *Foster Placements: Why They Succeed and Why They Fail.* London: Jessica Kingsley Publishers.

Sinclair, R. (1998) 'Involving children in planning their care.' *Child and Family Social Work 3*, 137–142.

Sinclair, R., Cronin, K., Lanyon, C., Stone, V. and Hulusi, A. (2002) *Aim High, Stay Real: Outcomes for Children and Young People: The Views of Children, Parents and Professionals.* London: Children and Young People's Unit.

Sinclair, R. and Franklin, A. (2000) *Young People's Participation, Quality Protects Research Briefing No 3.* London: DOH.

Skinner, B.F. (1953) *Science and Human Behaviour.* New York: Macmillan.

Sloper, P. (2000) *User-friendly Information for Families with Disabled Children: A Guide to Good Practice.* York: York Publishing Services.

Smart, C., Neale, B. and Wade, A. (2001) *The Changing Experience of Childhood: Families and Divorce.* Cambridge: Policy Press.

Social Work Task Force (2009) *Building a Safe and Confident Future.* London: DCSF.

Starkey, F. (2003) '"The Empowerment Debate": consumerist, professional and liberational perspectives in health and social care.' *Social Policy and Society 2*, 4, 273–284.

Strickland-Clark L., Campbell, D. and Dallos, R. (2000) 'Children's and adolescent's views on family therapy.' *Journal of Family Therapy 22*, 3, 324–341.

The Fostering Network (1999) *UK National Standards for Foster Care.* Available at www.fosteringresources.co.uk/resources/publications/uk-national-standards-foster-care, accessed on 13 June 2011.

The Prince's Trust (2007) *The Cost of Exclusion: Counting the cost of youth disadvantage in the UK.* London: The Prince's Trust. Available at www.princes-trust.org.uk/PDF/Princes%20Trust%20Research%20Cost%20of%20Exclusion%20apr07.pdf, accessed on 20 June 2011.

Thoburn, J., Lewis, A. and Shemmings, D. (1995) *Paternalism or Partnership? Family Involvement in the Child Protection Process.* London: HMSO.

Thomas, N. (2002) *Children, Family and the State: Decision Making in Child Participation.* Bristol: Policy Press.

Thomas, N. (2005) 'Has anything really changed? Managers' views of looked after children's participation in 1997 and 2004.' *Adoption and Fostering 29,* 1, 67–77.

Thomas, N. and O'Kane, C. (1998) 'The ethics of participatory research with children.' *Children and Society 12,* 336–348.

Thomas, N. and O'Kane, C. (1999) 'Children's participation in reviews and planning meetings when they are looked after in middle childhood.' *Child and Family Social Work 4,* 221–230.

Thomas, C. and Thomas, N. (eds) (2005) 'Listening to children.' *Adoption and Fostering 29,* 1–119.

Thompson, D. A. (2002) *Bullying: Effective Strategies for Long Term Improvement.* London: Routledge-Falmer.

Timms, J. and Thoburn, J. (2003) *Your Shout! A Survey of the Views of 706 Children and Young People in Public Care.* London: NSPCC.

Tregeagle, S. (2006) *Use of Information and Communication Technology by Families using Barnardo's Australia.* Australia: Barnardo's.

Tregeagle, S. and Darcy, M. (2008) 'Child welfare and information and communication technology: today's challenge.' *British Journal of Social Work 38,* 8, 1481–1498.

Treseder, P. (1997) *Empowering Children and Young People.* London: Children's Rights Office and Save the Children.

Triangle/NSPCC (2001) *Two Way Street: Communicating with Disabled Children and Young People Video Pack.* Leicester: NSPCC.

Triangle/NSPCC (2002) *How is it? An Image Vocabulary for Children About Feelings, Rights and Safety, Personal Care and Sexuality.* Leicester: NSPCC.

UN Committee on the Rights of the Child (CRC), *General Comment No. 12 (2009): The right of the child to be heard,* 20 July 2009, CRC/C/GC/12. Available at www.unhcr.org/refworld/docid/4ae562c52.html. Accessed 23 March 2011.

UNICEF (2003) *The State of the World's Children.* New York: UNICEF.

UNICEF (2005) *Child Labour Today.* London: UNICEF.

UNICEF (2007a) *Childhood in Industrialised Countries.* London: UNICEF.

UNICEF (2007b) *Childhood in Perspective: An Overview of Child Wellbeing.* Florence: Innocenti, Research Centre.

United Nations (1989) *Convention on the Rights of the Child.* Geneva: United Nations

Utting, W. (1997) *People Like Us: The Report of the Review of Safeguards for Children Living Away from Home.* London: HMSO.

van der Zee, B. (2010) 'Tuition fees school walkout: "We need to have our voices heard".' *The Guardian,* 19 November.

Vis, S. and Thomas, N. (2009) 'Beyond talking: children's participation in Norwegian care and protection cases.' *European Journal of Social Work 12,* 2, 155–168.

Wade, H., Lawton, A. and Stevenson, M. (2001) *Hear by Right: Setting Standards for the Active Involvement of Young People in Local Democracy.* Local Government Association. London and Leicester: National Youth Agency.

Wade, J. (2003) *Leaving Care. Quality Protects Research Briefing 7.* Dartington: DOH.

Walker, S. (1999) 'Children's Perspectives on Attending Statutory Reviews.' In D. Shemmings (ed.) *Involving Children in Family Support and Child Protection.* London: HMSO.

Ward, A. (2008) 'Real-time Communication in Residential Care.' In B. Luckock and M. Lefevre (eds) *Direct Work: Social Work with Children and Young People in Care.* London: BAAF.

Ward, L. (1997) *Seen and Heard: Involving Disabled Children and Young People in Research and Development Projects.* York: Joseph Rowntree Foundation.

Watson, J.B. (1924) *Psychology from the Standpoint of a Behaviourist.* Philadelphia: Lippencott.

Webb, S. (2006) 'Children's Participation in Child Protection Conferences.' Presentation at ISPCAN and BASPCAN congress, York.

Webster Stratton, C. and Hancock, L. (1998) 'Parent Training for Parents of Young Children with Conduct Problems: Content, Methods and Therapeutic Processes.' In C.E. Scaefer and J. Breismeister (eds) *Handbook of Parent Training.* New York: Wiley.

Wesson, M. and Salmon, K. (2001) 'Drawing and showing: helping children to report emotionally laden events.' *Applied Cognitive Psychology 15,* 3, 301–320.

Whilet, B. and Tjandraningsih, I. (1998) *Child Workers in Indonesia.* Bandung: AKATIGA.

White, S., Hall, C. and Peckover, S. (2009) 'The descriptive tyranny of the common assessment framework: technologies of categorisation and professional practice in child welfare.' *British Journal of Social Work 39,* 7, 1197–1217.

Who Cares? Trust (1998) *Remember My Messages.* London: Who Cares? Trust.

Wilcox, R. (1991) *Family Decision Making: Family Group Conferences: Practitioners Views.* Lower Hutt, New Zealand: Practitioners Publishing.

Williams, C. (2005) 'A critical evaluation of hierarchical representations of community involvement: some lessons from the UK.' *Community Development Journal 40,* 10, 30–38.

Williams, F. (2004) 'What matters is what works: why every child matters to New Labour. Commentary on the Department for Education and Skills Green Paper.' *Every Child Matters, Critical Social Policy 24,* 406–427.

Williams, F. and Churchill, H. (2006) *Empowering Parents in Sure Start Local Programmes: National Evaluation of Sure Start Report.* London: DfES.

Williamson, B. (2003) *The Grit in the Oyster: Final Report of the Evaluation on Investing in Children.* Durham: Durham University.

Willow, C. (2002) *Participation in Practice: Children and Young People as Partners in Change.* London: The Children's Society.

Wilson, K. and Bell, M. (2001) *Evaluating Family Group Conferences: A Report on a Family Group Conference Pilot Project.* York: University of York.

Wilson, K. and Bell, M. (2003) 'Ask the Family.' *Community Care,* 27 February.

Wright, J.K. (2004) 'Developing On-line Text-based Counselling in the Workplace.' In C. Bolton, C. Howlett, C. Lago and J. Wright (eds) *Writing Cures: An Introductory Handbook of Writing in Counselling and Therapy.* Hove: Brunner-Routledge.

Wright, P. and Haydon, D. (2002) *'Taking Part' Toolkit: Promoting the Real Participation of Children and Young People.* Manchester: North West Children's Taskforce.

Wright, P., Turner, C., Clay, D. and Mills, H. (2006) *The Participation of Children and Young People in Developing Social Care.* Participation Practice Guide 2006. London: Social Care Institute for Excellence.

Subject Index

Author Index